ATTITUDE

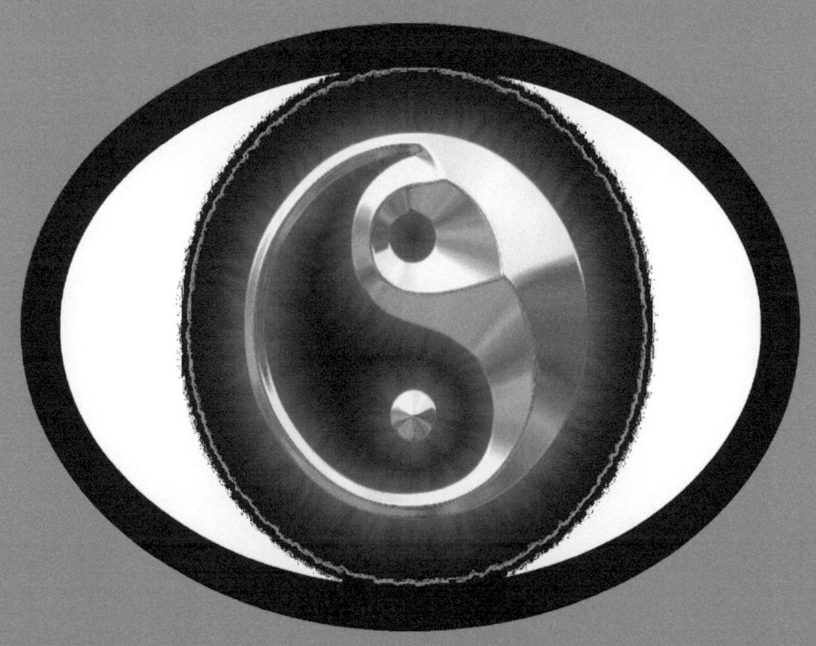

Samuel Blankson

ISBN: 1-4116-2382-7

Acknowledgements

Thanks to God, for giving me the sense to choose to live with a positive mental attitude. Thanks to my wife, Uju, for lovingly reminding me of this choice daily.

Thanks to the many authors of inspirational books and audio material who have helped me keep my attitude positive through the years.

Contents

Introduction

Today, we are blessed with the many benefits of modern technology. We can know of events around the world, as they occur, we can travel around the globe in less than a day, and we can communicate instantly, accurately, and reliably with, almost anyone, anywhere we choose.

Far from increasing our happiness, contentment, and enjoyment of life, most of us are unhappy, ungrateful, impatient, dissatisfaction, frustrated and estranged from our fellow men and women.

The views we hold of our lives and our world are tainted with distrust, resentment, and negative attitudes. Each hour, the world media churns out material to feed this negativity, through its printing presses and television and satellite stations.

The situation has reached crisis point, we no longer know what a positive mental attitude is, let alone how to escape our negative thought patterns, in order to search, find, and apply a positive attitude to our thoughts and actions.

This book tackles the monumental task of redefining your mental attitude, setting it to a positive polarity, and maintaining this polarity regardless of the negative media bombardment, and the challenges of modern day life.

Samuel Blankson

Chapter 1

- ***What is your mental attitude?***

What Is Your Mental Attitude?

Your mental attitude is a complex mental state involving your beliefs, your feelings, your values, and your disposition to act in a certain way. The following four attributes makeup your mental attitude:

- Feelings
- Beliefs
- Values
- Disposition to act

Attributes Of Mental Attitude

These attributes will shape your mental attitude, and through this, affect and control your experience of life.

To gain a better understanding of what your mental attitude comprises of, you will have to understand each of these attributes.

Feelings

By having an intuitive understanding of something, you are said to have a feeling about it. These feelings do not require any justification or proof by logical, and or other means. Therefore you can hold feelings on illogical, unfounded and in some cases, ridiculous ideas and notions.

Often the intuitive part of feelings is questionable. Sometimes stubbornness can cause you to claim to hold an intuitive understanding, when you may not have such intuition about the subject matter.

Feelings are a great way of experiencing and applying intuition, however, when this tool is misused, it can stain your life with negativity. For instance; feeling that everyone is out to get you or feeling that you are worthless, undeserving of love, or a myriad of other negative feelings, can hold you back from fully experiencing life and adding to the beautiful mural of your life.

Beliefs

Beliefs are cognitive content held as true, in other words, a set of thoughts you hold to be true, becomes your beliefs. These thoughts do not need to be true or false to become beliefs. The only prerequisite for thoughts to be converted into belief is that you believe in them. For instance, if you believe that walking under a ladder is bad luck, you will avoid doing so even if you are inconvenienced for taking this action. Your beliefs, however unfounded, will be true to you, and you will behave accordingly. You can tell by your actions, speech and thoughts on any subject, whether you believe in it or not.

Values

When feelings and beliefs are combined, values are created. Your values are beliefs that you have some emotional attachment to. This emotional attachment, need not be only for, but can also be against the belief.

The integrity and structure of a value often crumble when tested. Today Neuro-Linguistic Programming (NLP) masters and psychologists can help remove some of these values simply by introducing doubt in a belief, more on this later. Your values shape the way you see and treat life, therefore, by changing your feelings and beliefs you can alter your values and thus change your life.

Disposition to act

Others will first experience your values through your acts. By speaking, writing, or through action, you will reveal your values to others, and by them doing the same; they will allow you to experience their values. Having values allows you to select a course of action in many circumstances.

In fact, the stronger your values are on a subject; the easier it is to decide a course of action to take, concerning that subject. You only hesitate in decision making when there are conflicts in your values and beliefs, or when you hold no feelings, beliefs, or values on a subject.

As an example, if you tend to raise your voice whenever you are in a debate or argument. You may have a feeling that you are not listened to in such situations (this could be intuitive or it could be based on a belief about how the person you are arguing with perceives you). Your value in this example may be that, in general, you are not respected by people, a particular group (children, the opposite sex, parents, teachers etc), or a particular individual. This value could result in you developing the disposition to raise your voice in such situations.

In the example above, you can see how the feeling of not being heard, can lead to the development of a belief about the listener, and a value of not being respected, resulting in a disposition to shout or raise your voice in circumstances when you feel you are not being listened to.

This is not the only combination of feelings, beliefs, and values that will create the disposition to raise your voice. In this book, we are primarily interested in feelings, beliefs, values, and dispositions to act that aid, or hinder the acquisition of a positive mental attitude.

If you allow your feelings, beliefs, values and disposition to act, to be negatively biased towards yourself, others, and the world, you will live with a negative mental attitude.

Cynicism, pessimism, and a dozen other words, describe attitudes of mind to avoid. You shall look closely at developing a state of mind that steers you far from the negative feelings, beliefs, values, and dispositions to act that lead to negative mental attitudes.

Polarity

Most things in nature exhibit a duality, hot and cold, birth and death, etc. Your mental attitude is no different in this sense. It can be positive or negative.

It takes work to make your attitude positive, just as it takes energy to make a kettle boil. Like the kettle, you cannot remove the energy and expect the kettle to continue boiling, neither can you neglect your mind and expect it to stay positive.

This polarity begins to shift towards positivism when you associate pleasure with people, situations, and things. Conversely, by associating pain and displeasure with the same people, situations, and things, you will move your mental attitudes' polarity towards negativism.

By changing, and maintaining the polarity of your mental attitude, you will change your experience of life.

Let us look at the two poles in the continuum of your mental attitude. It is called here, a continuum, because there is no black and white to this bias.

For instance, if you were standing near molten lava whilst boiling a kettle you would hardly call that water hot. Whilst the touch of a hand at room temperature in the midst of a Siberian snowstorm could be considered, hot.

Like these two examples, the polarity of your mental attitude is relative. If you live, work and play amongst chronic sufferers of negative mental attitude, your slight bias to positive over their mental attitudes' polarity, could fool you to think you had a positive mental attitude. However, remove yourself from that negative environment and attend a highly charged motivational rally, or conference and you would feel like your mental attitude was at the end of the negative pole.

To determine whether your mental attitude is positive or negatively biased, you have to consider what you are comparing with it. Let us take a close look at negative and positive attitudes, and from this, you can accurately determine when you are leaning too far into the negative realm.

Negative

There are several attributes to a negative mental attitude. Firstly, the negative mind lacks faith and positive hope. Secondly, a mind steeped in negativity lacks self-love. Let us see how these two traits affect your mind negatively.

Faith and Hope

Throughout your life, you may encounter things that seem unfair, or wrong. When things go wrong in your life, you may question your faith in the Creator, or the intrinsic goodness of your fellow men. If you do not satisfactorily answer these questions, and reclaim your faith in the Creator, and the human race, you will become bitter, fearful, jealous, resentful, or a wide variety of other negative states.

Self love

When you are not proud, happy, satisfied, and content with yourself as a human being, you will have the tendency to, either, abuse yourself, or abuse others. Constantly putting yourself or others down because of your inadequacies will only further negate your mental attitude. As the saying goes "if you don't love yourself, how can you love others?"

Positive

The attributes that aid a positive mental attitude are gratefulness, joy, faith, and hope. By living with gratefulness, faith, and hope, you will be happy, and want to share your joy. Let us look further into each of these attributes.

Faith and Hope

You will live in positive hope by believing and having faith in a higher power, a Creator who truly loves you, who only wants the ultimate good for you. Problems will not seem so insurmountable within this positive hope, and you will feel an inner sense of knowing that all will be well in the end.

Gratefulness

Gratefulness comes from understanding how lucky you are to be alive, and have whatever life you may be living now. Because of hope in your future, you will know that something better is ahead for you, and thus you will take each breath, and live each day with a sense of thankfulness. It is impossible to be grateful and negative at the same time. True gratefulness can only exist in a positive mind; therefore, by developing a sense of gratefulness, you will swing your mind further into the positive realm.

Chapter 2

- ***Causes of your negative mental attitude***

Causes of your negative mental attitude

There are many reasons that will cause you to develop a negative mental attitude. None of us is born with a negative mental attitude. We develop a negative mental attitude through our choices; made after exposure to life's events, situations and our environment. The following are the major causes of the development of a negative mental attitude:

- Loss of faith or loss of hope.
- Lack of purpose.
- Negative associations.

You shall now take a closer look at each of these points.

Loss Of Faith Or Hope

When you lose faith in God, your fellow human family, the world, or yourself, you begin to associate negativity to things in your life that remind you of the cause of this loss of faith. Often you may not loose all your faith, but you may loose hope. This alone will be enough to turn your attitude towards negativity. Let us look at some of the causes of faith and hope loss.

Disappointments

Disappointments occur when your expectations of an outcome are not fully met. When you expect something to happen in your life, and it does not happen, you will become disappointed. Depending on the importance you placed on the disappointing outcome, you will set the level of negativity in your mind. As an example, a child who is expecting a desired toy for Christmas, and who is disappointed, may develop a negative mental attitude towards Christmas, his or her parents or Santa.

Loss

When you grow attached to something, or someone, loosing this attachment will be very painful. Feelings of being lost, unfairness, frustration, anger, blame, and resentment can lead you to want revenge, harbour bitterness, cynicism and hate, display violence or other antisocial behaviour.

Loss can cause your attitude to slip into negativism. Remembering that loss is inevitable in life will steer you through these times. Being spiritually grounded, having faith in a higher power, having loved ones and caring friends around you at these times is the best way of staying positive through these times of grief.

Often being the one that others depend on for support and strength during these periods is enough to keep your attitude and spirits up. However, putting off the grieving process will only channel it through other sources. This channelling of your pent up grief will normally manifest through negative means. In this scenario, it is important to remember to take time to grieve. Those you supported through their grieving will in turn be there for you when you need them.

After each loss, you will go through a loss cycle. This cycle of loss is as follows:

- Shock – you cannot believe it has happened.
- Depression – you feel sorry for yourself for having the loss.
- Anger – you blame yourself or others for the loss.
- Reconciliation – you come to an understanding of the cause of the loss, and you understand it from many perspectives.
- Forgiveness – you forgive yourself and others for the loss.

This cycle is inevitable, and you must go through it to heal properly. The time it takes to go through this cycle, will be different for each person, and for each loss. You can speedup your recovery by willingly embracing each phase of the loss cycle. Not doing so will prolong your time in that phase.

Loss is a reminder of how precious every moment in life is. Do not waste this gift. Share your love with all those you meet, and remember to regularly show, and tell your loved ones how much you love them.

Health

When you are ill or unhealthy, your vigilance in maintaining your positive attitude is greatly reduced. You may loose hope, or falter in your faith. You are inclined to display impatience and be disagreeable.

Although achievable, maintaining a positive mental attitude whilst ill, is more difficult than whilst you are well, and healthy. Therefore, it is wise to maintain a healthy lifestyle in order to avoid getting ill or being unhealthy. If you are healthy most of the time, you will not need to worry about maintaining your attitude during bouts of ill health.

If you are unavoidably ill for long periods, seek to be grateful for what you do have, and still enjoy. It is during these times that your faith and spiritual support become invaluable.

Lack Of Purpose

Mediocrity

Doing enough, just to get by, not excelling at anything, never going the extra mile, being average, will earn you a life of mediocrity. Mediocrity is a state that you fall into when you do not pursue an ideal, dream, vision, or goal. Mediocre people lack purpose in their lives. Because they lack purpose, they do not strive for anything. They are alive but not living. They are the living dead.

Avoid being mediocre. Dream, plan, set goals, and go after them with all your spirit, energy, and enthusiasm. Always seek to excel at what ever you are doing. Give more than is expected, and you will get more than was promised.

Goals are objectives with an expected achievement date, and an associate reward. Get a dream or vision, and use goals to achieve them.

The road to success is fraught with disappointments, frustrations, and setbacks. However, when you overcome all these, the road to success promises fulfilment, contentment, joy, pride, self-improvement, mental toughness and will power, self-mastery, wealth, happiness and self-respect, to name a few..

Poverty

Poverty is a reality for the vast majority of the world's population. For these people, there is a lack of opportunity, education, resources, and help to improve their circumstances. At best they can pray, work hard, seek to educate themselves, set goals and work towards moving out of their helpless state, and hope things will change.

For those of you fortunate enough to have education, health services, and career opportunities available to you, there is simply no excuse.

Every year immigrants, refugees and other foreigners fleeing from their countries arrive on the shores of western countries. On average, these people excel, and in a phenol-menally short time, become property owners, business owners, and highly educated individuals.

These people prove each year that, given the opportunities available to you, success is achievable in a short period. Yet in these western countries, there are people exposed to the same opportunities who choose to live in poverty. They can get educated, but choose not to. They can get work, and build careers, but choose indolence and dependence on the state. They can excel in all aspects of their lives, but choose to, instead, just survive.

Do not allow yourself to fall into this category. Seek to better yourself and your life. If you are uneducated, seek to get educated. If underpaid, you should seek to find employment that rewards hard work, enthusiasm, and loyalty. Work hard and you will soon enjoy a better state of living.

Change your environment and associations to help you in this endeavour. You will find out more on associations in the next section.

Scarcity thinking

The world has provided untold wealth to countless people and civilisations, yet except light radiation from the stars, our own sun and moon, and the odd meteor, nothing has being added to this planet for countless millennia. All the wealth enjoyed by our world, and all previous civilisations, have been from the transferral of matter and energy, from one source to another.

This profound fact, tells you that there is a limitless abundance in our world. Taking from this abundance will not diminish what others can take. The giving of a smile is a good example of this. When you smile, you loose nothing. By smiling often, you are not diminishing the world smiles reserve. Yet some people are so reluctant to share their smile.

Many are afraid to share their wealth, possessions, and success, for the fear of loosing or diminishing their supply. They have scarcity thinking. Scarcity thinking generates a negative mental attitude. They believe there is a limited supply of wealth and success in the world. Thus, they think by sharing theirs, others will surpass them whilst they will fall behind.

By sharing your success, you only become more successful. By giving your help, advice, and support, you become a happier, more fulfilled person. Test this for yourself. When do you enjoy material possessions the most? When you keep them to yourself, or when you share them with others? The answer is, when you share. Everything is more enjoyable when shared.

Rid yourself of scarcity thinking by learning to share, and help others to achieve and enjoy what you have achieved.

By doing this, more will be apportioned to you, in different, and rewarding ways.

Materialism

Believing that your material possessions alone will make you happy in life will lead you not to value others, and yourself. You will put material things above human life and human relationships. The truth is that life is human relationships. Getting along with others, valuing the times you share with them, and having others, is one of the keys to a successful life.

Putting material possessions above human life will have you disrespect, and undervalue others. These are effects of a negative mental attitude towards human life. This will cause others to dislike you in turn, and see you as being materialistic and shallow.

You will not gain happiness without believing in a higher power, loving yourself, loving others, and being grateful for what you have. Materialism will have you constantly seeking the new thing, in order to feel a fleeting sense of happiness.

If you stop to think about your possessions, you will realise that, you enjoy them the most when you share them with others. When you keep your material possessions to yourself, you only receive a fraction of the pleasure you could gain by sharing them with others.

Therefore, share your wealth, help others, and enjoy your possessions with friends and family. Do not lord your material possessions over others. Do not live a life, cantered on having the latest thing, where your happiness and your self-image are defined by your material possessions. Being materialistic in this way, will corrupt and erode your positive attitude, and cause you to have short highs, and prolonged lows in your attitude and happiness.

Ignorance

Ignorance breeds fear and hatred. Being ignorant will lead you to cause negative attitudes in others, and yourself. By not understanding something, or someone, can lead you to make false assumptions. These assumptions, when negative, will cause you to react and treat the things, and people you do not understand with fear, contempt, hatred, or a myriad of negative reactions, all stemming from having a negative mental attitude.

Today, most of the world's problems stem from ignorance. Not understanding others' way of life has caused many to treat others with disdain, contempt, and disregard. This negative treatment and attitude towards others has led to misunderstandings, conflict, war, and death.

The best way to eradicate ignorance from your life is to show love towards all others. Understanding that, from their point of view you are the stranger, or strange one, will allow you to treat others with consideration, understanding, and respect. Treat others as you would have them treat you, and you will avoid the negative results of ignorance.

Ignorance also manifests itself in many kinds of folly. Lack of wisdom and understanding are the route causes of this type of ignorance.

Seek to educate yourself. Travel widely, and experience different peoples, cultures, and experiences. Seek constantly, to add to your knowledge by studying subjects in which you lack knowledge. Associate with wise and knowledgeable people, and you too will grow in wisdom and knowledge.

Association

Media, negative associations and negative environments

It has been said by some wise men that, "we are all the sum of the books we read, recordings we listen to, and people we associate with". If this is the case, then the literature, media, and your human associations make up a very large proportion of who you will become.

If you have children, you try to control their associations so that they do not hang out with the bad influences of society. Similarly, it is wise to control the sources of association you, as an adult, are exposed.

Today, we associate with people in many ways. Some are direct person to person, others are less interactive (i.e. television, newspapers and magazines, videos and DVD's, letters, telephone, and through the various methods offered by the internet (video conferencing, chat, email etc)

You must filter out the negatives from all your associations, whether through what you read, watch or through your personal relationships.

Your environment

Your environment will affect you, directly or indirectly. If you are exposed to an environment that makes you feel unhappy, miserable, stressed, anxious, fearful, inadequate, or drained of positive energy, your attitude will also be affected.

You can see this in action by observing the people at your place of work, and observing people on holiday. You will notice the holiday group are smiling more, talking more, sharing more, and generally feeling good with themselves and others. The environment at your work place may be the opposite of the holiday environment. In the work environment, people may be quieter, more introverted, fearful to be noticed by their boss, fearful of sharing in case others surpass them, and unwilling to smile because they do not feel happy to be at work.

You can see the results of over exposure to this negative environment, in your colleagues who have been at the job for a longer period than you have.

This example highlights only one of many negative environments you will be exposed to in your lifetime. Insuring these negative environments do not affect your attitude is crucial to being happy and successful.

Chapter 3

- ***Acquiring a positive mental attitude***

Acquiring A Positive Mental Attitude

Your positive mental attitude comes from associations of pleasure with events, situations, things, or people. By associating pleasure with things, and people in your life, you will develop, and exhibit a positive mental attitude towards them.

The Non-Physical

Some intangible feelings and mindsets automatically generate positive mental attitudes. These are as follows:

> **Gratefulness** – cultivate a sense of gratefulness for all the things you have and enjoy today, like your mind, body, health, family, friends, children, spouse, job, sunshine, food, etc. If any of the things that you already have, but are taking for granted, were to be taken from you, your life would be far worse than it is now. Therefore, be grateful for every blessing in your life.
>
> **Activeness** – stay active and healthy. Engage in regular exercises. You can jog, cycle, swim, join a gym, join a sports team, or simply go for walks. Activeness keeps you fit and healthy, it allows the waste from your cells to be circulated through your lymphatic system, keeping your cells healthier and less polluted.
>
> Activities that get your heart pumping at higher rates also help prevent heart problems, by keeping your heart stronger and healthier. Exercising, also allows vast amounts of oxygen to be introduced to the body through deeper breathing. This helps your cells stay healthy and nourished.
>
> Finally, an active life helps you burn more calories and convert fat into energy, thus helping to maintain your

ideal body weight. When you are active, you are happier and therefore your mental attitude will be more positive.

Ambition – you have to have the desire to achieve more. Without this desire or ambition, you will not plan, work, or take action to achieve anything. No ambition will result in no goals and no purpose. A life without purpose will be death to any success.

Hard work – hard work is its own reward. This saying is true in many ways. Here are a few of the rewards of hard work:

1. Keeps you active.
2. Makes you feel good about yourself.
3. Yields more success for you.
4. Allows you to do more.
5. Allows you to learn more.
6. Makes you proud of your achievements.
7. Will have you recognised over other less industrious colleagues.
8. Will develop the work ethic within you.
9. Will allow you to set a good example for your children, friends, family, and colleagues.

To work hard, simply do what is required before, or when it is required, to your best ability, in the shortest time possible. Always try to go the extra mile by giving more than is expected.

Purpose and goal – get a purpose, set goals, and take action to achieve your goals. Doing this will greatly improve your positive mental attitude. Without a purpose, you do not feel like living, you do not feel alive and you do not feel hopeful, happy, or necessary in life.

Learn to convert your dreams into objectives. Plan how you will achieve these objectives within a deadline date, and assign an appropriate reward to each goal. Only when you successfully achieve the goal, must you give yourself the reward. Setting goals, and working on achieving them by a deadline date, will bring focus into your life, and your attitude will change for the better when you are working on achieving a desired goal.

Consult my book, *Planning and Goal Setting* for more detailed information on goal setting and planning techniques.

Association – having negative associations can cause you to have a negative attitude. Conversely, positive associations will result in your having a positive mental attitude. Let us now look at the various associations you currently access.

Newspapers

If you currently read a tabloid newspaper that is full of gossip, lies, sensationalistic and biased views, you are only harming yourself. You are warping your image of the world, and thus, warping the image you have of yourself in this world. If what you read and watch is mainly focussed on the negative aspects of human nature (as most news programming nowadays is), you will create cynicism, mistrust and fear within yourself. This will affect your attitude for the worse.

Avoid the trashy newspapers and immoral periodicals depicting sex and violence, as well as those promoting weaker moral values. Associating with these types of magazines and newspapers will corrupt your character, and harm your attitude.

Television

Today, you do not have to sit through the negative that some television programs churn out, soap operas with negative and unrealistic storylines, depicting a world of sordid and immoral behaviour that, if you associate with long enough, will change your values and your life.

Programs that attempt to shock with sex, or violence, will leave their scar on your attitude if you associate with them long enough.

You need not consume bland senseless programming aimed at filling gaps in television program slots. These shows are banal, and in many cases idiotic. These types of programming can be found late at night or during Friday evenings on various television channels.

You can choose to subscribe to channels that will stimulate, educate, and entertain you, without having to lower your values, morals, integrity, and mental attitude. If you subscribe to cable or satellite television, you will be able to select, from hundreds of channels, those that best match your values and morals.

Even with so much choice, be sure to observe the following rules:

1. Use your VCR, or other television-recording device, to record programs that fit your moral and ethical standards, as well as being educational, entertaining, and positive. You will be able to watch these recorded programs when you find nothing good on television to watch. This will stop you settling for any garbage and thus corrupting your mind and attitude.
2. Get balance in your television viewing; aim to watch a balance of educational and informative, entertaining as well as spiritually uplifting films, and shows.

3. Avoid shows with excessive sex, violence, and immoral behavioural content.

Books

Whilst literary works can contain some of the most enlightened and uplifting contents, there are those that contain dangerous and warped notions. Avoid reading books that promote racial bigotry, hatred, violence, and self-abuse through excesses in sex, violence, and drugs. These books will affect you in a profoundly negative way. They will cause you to re-evaluate your morals, ethics, and spiritual beliefs.

A study of the way your mind works will reveal to you the importance of controlling what goes into yours. Whatever you think about the most, will begin to manifest in your life. This is true even if you are living in fear of something. That something will manifest, and control your life. Therefore, be vigilant in controlling what you read, watch, and listen to.

Music

Music is unique to the human animal, and is enjoyed and loved by all. Nothing is so easy to constantly associate with, as music can be. It is pervasive, and finds itself into every aspect of our lives. This pervasiveness makes negative music so dangerous.

Even when you do not consciously listen to the lyrics of songs, your subconscious mind will hear and act on them. Therefore, it is vital that you check what you listen. Songs that contain abusive language, sex, violence, as well as those promoting an immoral lifestyle are abundant today. They are on the television, in our streets, in the restaurants and shops we visit, as well as on the radio internet and thus in our minds.

If you do not filter these negative lyrics out of your mind, they will take root and change your attitude without you being aware of it.

To combat this bombardment of negative music in your life, do the following:

- Keep a selection of positive music in your car, and listen to these rather than to the radio.
- Listen only to the radio stations that offer a playing list that is inline with your faith, ethics, and morals.
- If you are on the move, use a personal music, player with headphones, rather than listening to the music offered by the retail stores and other places you frequent.
- If you have children, monitor the lyrics in the songs they listen to, and try to steer them from sexually immoral, violence promoting and abusive music.

Interpersonal relationships

As you have learned, you are affected by what you watch, read, and hear. However, of all these things, none is more dangerous to your attitude than the company you keep.

Your family, friends, and colleagues will affect you easier, quicker, and more so, than any other type association. Be on your guard against negative influences in this area. Avoid people who make you feel down, and drained when you are with them. They are easy to spot and they may not be your friends.

Not so easy to pick out are negative friends. Because they are your friends, you will make allowances for their beliefs and behaviour, even when negative. However, these beliefs and behaviour will rub off on you over time. If your friends are in the habit of deriding you or putting your down, talk to them about stopping this behaviour. If the behaviour persists, distance yourself from them, and find, or make other friends who will support and uplift you.

Avoid relationships that contain jealousy, hatred, envy, mistrust, and lies. If your friend is jealous, or envious of you, how can they be genuinely supportive, and encouraging to you, through difficult times? If that is how they really feel, you will find that they are either glad of your plight, or were involved in its creation. You need to replace your negative friends with quality friends who are really rooting for you, and who always wish you the best.

This may seem harsh, and may be difficult for you, but remembered this; it is quality, not quantity of friendships, you want in your life. Any one who is not uplifting and positive will be a drain on you in the long term. This will lower your self-esteem and damage your self-image, causing you to have a negative mental attitude.

If you find it a challenge to make new friends, consult the following books:

- *How to win friends and influence people*
  by Dale Carnegie
- *Making friends*
  by Andrew Matthews
- *How to improve your confidence*
  by Dr Kenneth Hambly
- *How to start a conversation and make friends*
  by Don Gabor

Your interpersonal relationships can produce some of the most rewarding, and challenging associations that you can have. Therefore, seek to make yours rewarding through selecting quality friends who will help you grow in self-esteem, and who will help you develop a positive attitude.

Positive memories – seek to experience happy memories, and recall them whenever your mental attitude is slipping towards the negative. Replay those happy memories repeatedly in your mind to recreate those feelings of happiness. Memories of joy, happiness, humour, achievement, and success should be recalled and savoured regularly.

Youthfulness – have a childlike attitude. This means being more playful, dreaming, imagining, being in awe of new and wonderful things, having a sense of adventure, having fun, smiling, and laughing more. All these things will help you have a positive mental attitude. We are all children in adult bodies. You may know more than you did as a child, but do not loose your childlike innocence by taking your life too seriously. When you remember to play, laugh, and explore with your life, you will improve your positive attitude.

Self-esteem and self-image - the way you view and feel about yourself will greatly determine how you interact with others. It will also determine how deserving you feel. Deservedness will control the decisions you make, and the utilisation of opportunities. These two things alone can determine whether you are a success or a failure in your life.

It is therefore critical that you develop and maintain a healthy self-esteem and self-image. You shall now examine self-esteem and self-image in detail, and look at how you can develop and maintain yours to create a positive mental attitude.

Your thoughts - your negative thoughts may stem from your experiences or bad situations. Perhaps you think you are overweight or unattractive. If you were put down in your past about your figure or looks, these put downs can follow you throughout your life, and manifest in a low self-esteem. This low self-esteem will negatively affect your mental attitude.

These thoughts, if not checked, will continue to plague you, even when the origin or cause of the thoughts has disappeared from your life. It becomes like a recording, constantly repeating, and replaying the same thoughts in your head until your self-esteem and self-confidence lies in tatters.

Regular repetition of any thought will develop into a belief. Whilst negative thoughts can cause you to feel like a failure, or make you feel inadequate, beliefs will make sure you fail, and fail consistently. We shall look at beliefs next.

Your beliefs - your thoughts create beliefs. Your beliefs are powerful things. Your beliefs determine how you see your world. They determine how you feel about things, and they control your attitude and value system.

By changing your beliefs concerning yourself, others, and your world, you will literally, change your attitude towards these things for the better.

Belief, like attitude, has a relative polarity of negative and positive. Because belief is a continuum, these poles are relative. Therefore, the boundaries of your belief poles will depend on where you are in the belief continuum.

If you are already very negative, your positive belief pole may already start within somebody's extreme negative pole. Therefore, your positive will be somebody's negative, and your negative will be somebody's positive.

It is therefore, only possible to work to improve your beliefs according to your current position in the belief continuum. It would be fruitless and frustrating to compare your beliefs with anybody else's, as you are not them, and you are not in the same position in the belief continuum as them.

Your beliefs can stem from a negative event or situation. These may often be rooted in the past, and you may not recall why you have the negative belief, but the belief will stay with you and grow as long as you feed it, by using it, and regularly calling on it.

Some events or situations will lead you to worry and feel anxiety and stress. Your bad experience in this case, will make you try to avoid these events or situations from ever occurring again. You may worry about them reoccurring and therefore, cause your attitude to slip into the negative, and your belief system to develop a protective shield to defend you from this future fear.

This protective shield could be in the form of you emotionally shutting off, or never trusting the opposite sex again etc. These beliefs will greatly limit your experience of life, and will shut you off from ever experiencing the joys and happiness that a successful life could bring you.

Belief work is very personal, and relative, only to the individual carrying out the improvements. To start, you have to change your thoughts about yourself, others, and your world.

Changing these thoughts will change your attitudes of thought. Often changing your attitude concerning a particular person, situation, occurrence, object, or event, will change your thoughts and your beliefs on the subject.

For example, if you hate rainy days, but live in a part of the world where it rains most of the time, you may feel depressed and miserable most of the time. If you are unable to relocate to a sunnier region, you can change your attitude towards the rain.

Self-talk - we all talk to ourselves all day long. The words you use when you talk to yourself may often be uncomplimentary. If these words are used regularly, you will begin to develop belief in them, and they will shape your self-esteem and self-image, causing your attitude to change also. If these negative self-descriptions continue, they will affect your attitude towards you.

Phrases such as "I am so clumsy", "I am so stupid, " "I always get things wrong", "trust me to mess things up", I cant do it", "I am broke", "I am useless", "I am ugly", "no one likes me", "I hate myself" etc, will not improve your self-esteem and self-image.

Phrases such as "I can do it"", "I am getting better at this", "I love myself", "I am attractive" etc, will help improve your self-esteem and self-image. Regularly using these descriptors will change your attitude towards you, positively.

Your social skills - you may know someone who has very little social grace and skill. They may be vulgar, rude and offensive, argumentative and antagonistic, talk too much, or talk too loud. Others may be timid, socially clumsy, mumble their speech, avoid eye contact, are overly apologetic, are manipulative, or gossip.

Socially unacceptable and antisocial traits are all contributors to your self-image and self-esteem. Therefore, it is vital that you develop, or change your social skills and social behaviour to support your self-image and self-esteem. Making this positive change will also affect your attitude.

Your lack of integrity - if you are unreliable, disloyal, and fickle, a liar, and a cheat, no one will trust you. Although your lack of integrity may be less obvious to the casual observer, it will have a long lasting effect on your attitude. It is therefore important that you operate with integrity when dealing with yourself and others.

Improving your integrity will automatically improve your level of success in all fields. This is because, whilst people can make allowances for most of the points we have thus far covered, no one will make allowances for your lack of integrity, unless they also lack integrity.

You will fail in business, fail as a parent, fail in your personal relationships, and fail in your religious faith if you do not operate with integrity. Any success you experience through operating without integrity will be short lived.

Integrity is one of the fundamentals highlighted in all the worlds' religions as a necessity for the attainment of spiritual success. It is also a fundamental requirement in the attainment of all worthwhile long-term success. Therefore operate with integrity and your attitude will be affected positively.

The Physical

To develop a positive mental attitude, also work on the following areas:

Your smile – smile and you immediately feel positive. People who see your smile also tend to catch your attitude and smile back, becoming that bit more agreeable.

Your associations - your family, friends, colleagues, relatives, and the press and media constitute your associations. If negative environments can affect your attitude, your negative associations will definitely affect your attitude for the worse.

This is because your associations have more of an emotional influence over you. Because your associations have more influence over you emotionally, they can and do affect your attitude more.

Even though you may know your negative associations are not good for you, loyalty, a sense of belonging or fear could be stopping you from breaking away from them.

Not breaking away from bad associations will cost you true success, happiness and a positive attitude.

Your posture - have you noticed how you change your body's posture to represent your mood or thoughts? You will tend to slouch if you are tired or bored. Similarly, you will tend to sit on the edge of your seat, and lean forward when you are captivated or interested in something, or in what someone is be saying.

The strangest thing about your body posture is that you can experience feelings by assuming the body posture you normally assume when you are naturally experiencing these feelings.

Therefore, if you were bored and you adopt the position on the edge of your seat, leaning forward with interest, you would feel interested, and captivated by the previously boring conversation.

Your attitude shows up through your body posture. It is easy to spot someone with a negative attitude. Just look at how they walk with lack of confidence, stand in a slouch, enter a room tentatively, or shake hands with a weak, non-committal, wet fish handshake etc.

Similarly, a person with a positive attitude can be identified through the confident way they move, stand upright and firm, enter a room with self-assuredness, and shake hands with a firm handshake etc.

The person with an apparently, overly high self-esteem can also be identified through the way they walk smugly, stand arrogantly, enter a room self-importantly, and shake hands overbearingly. These traits also show up a negative mental attitude. This is a compensatory behaviour, consciously or subconsciously used by someone to mask a feeling of inadequacy in him or her.

Your body posture is often the first thing people see of you. This can give them an idea of what you think of yourself, and often is the basis for how they will treat you.

Your body posture also determines how you feel, therefore prolonged use of a particular group of postures will have you feeling a certain way most of the time. If, your main group of body postures are negative, i.e. unsure, bored, tired, uninterested, shy, scared, lazy or uncommitted, your attitudes will develop to represent this.

On the other hand, if you display a confident, self-assured, assertive, humble, and industrious posture, you will develop these traits and they will become part of your attitude.

To improve your attitude through your posture, simply adopt the physical posture of someone with a positive attitude. Do you remember Christopher Reeves in Superman? When he turned into superman, his posture and speech changed instantly. He stood up right, make eye contact when he spoke to people, walked self assuredly, and acted confidently.

The following are eight simple ways to improve your posture:

1. Stand up straight with your shoulders back and your chest confidently, forward.
2. Walk with confidence. Take long confident strides, when you walk.
3. When sitting, adopt a position of interest and confidence. Do not slough in your chair, instead sit up, and stay attentive. You can achieve this best by sitting at the edge of your chair and leaning towards the person or persons, you are conversing.
4. Look people in their eyes when you shake their hands, greet them, and during conversations with them.
5. Speak clearly. Do not mumble or speak so softly that others have to strain to hear you.
6. Assert yourself when necessary. You do not have to use physical strength to show that you are in

control. A simple calm, confident, self-assuredness will suffice.

7. Breathe deeply and calmly. Avoid shallow short breaths. When you breathe calmly, you become calmer.
8. Move with purpose. Avoid nervous actions like swallowing or fidgeting.

By adopting a positive confident posture, you will be treated differently, and seen differently by others. Adopting a positive self-assured posture will also improve your self-esteem.

Health – few things can cause you to develop a negative mental attitude more than poor health. When you feel poorly, you act poorly, communicate poorly, and behave poorly. Your senses become introverted. You focus mainly on yourself, your discomfort, and your disease.

It is during these times that you are the most susceptible to negative influences. These negative influences will cause you to have a poor mental attitude.

It is during these times of ill health that you should employ gratefulness the most. Be grateful for the times when you were healthy, the medical help you may be receiving, the loved ones that are by your side and your ability to say thank you to God for keeping you alive.

Avoid, and limit your times of ill health. Look after your health. Attain a balance of sleep, recreation, and work. Eat healthily (fresh fruit and vegetables, pulses, legumes and nuts), frequently drink clean, filtered water, and avoid:

- polluted air and water
- fatty foods
- excessive red meats,
- excessive alcohol
- drug abuse
- smoking
- unprotected sex and casual sex
- violent and dangerous sports and activities
- long working hours
- excessive stress
- dangerous places (high crime and violent areas, war zones, natural disaster zones etc)

Develop a regular exercise routine. This could involve going for long walks, cycling, jogging, swimming, or regularly playing other sports. You will be healthy as long as at least three times a week, you engage in sporting activities that allow your heart rate to beat at the aerobic[1] level for at least twenty minutes.

If you are committed and able to do more, then that is even better, however, avoid over exercising. Twenty to sixty minutes, three to five times a week is the recommendation. Over exercising will deteriorate your body and cause your health to suffer in the end.

Your personal hygiene - when your body odour, breath, or bodily cleanliness is socially unacceptable, you will find that you too will become socially unacceptable. Few things will affect your self-image more than personal hygiene.

---

[1] There are many complex and mathematical methods of working out your aerobic heart rate. As a simple rule, if you can hold a conversation whilst exercising, you are working within your aerobic rate. If you find it difficult to say a few words whilst exercising, then you are working in the anaerobic range. Avoid anaerobic exercising.

Your effectiveness in communicating, interacting socially, and being accepted by other people, will all be negatively affected if your personal hygiene is not kept at a high standard.

Often, the small things cost you the most. Body odour, bad breath, and general bodily cleanliness are some of these small things. In a job interview, they will cost you a job. In a relationship, they will cost you intimacy, and in your social interactions, they will make you an outcast and possibly the butt of jokes.

Here are a list of personal hygiene points to help improve your self-image and self-esteem, and thus your attitude:

1. Wash your whole body daily. Clean your nostrils and ears.
2. Brush your teeth at least every morning upon awakening. Use a mouthwash and include flossing in your regime. If you are unaware of any of these, then consult your dentist.
3. If you have an unruly beard or moustache, consult a barber or shave regularly.
4. If you suffer from dandruff in your hair, treat it with anti-dandruff shampoo.
5. Comb or brush your hair into a presentable state before leaving your abode.
6. Use an antiperspirant spray or stick under your arm. This need not be deodorised but is advisable especially if you suffer from body odour. The best underarm deodorant I know can be found at *www.pitrok.co.uk*. This natural solution works extremely well at suppressing body odours whilst allowing your body to perspire naturally. It is odourless and extremely long lasting.

7. Use a skin moisturiser to moisturise your skin, and apply balm to your lips if they tend to get dry during the day.
8. If you suffer from foot odour, treat your shoes with odour eaters or some other antifungal footwear treatment.
9. Carry around a mouth spray, especially if you enjoy garlic in your meals or if you smoke. Use this spray after meals or cigarettes before speaking, at close range, with people.
10. If you have a flatulence problem, consult a doctor or a chemist and take their advice concerning ending, or controlling your flatulence problem.
11. If your nails are jagged from biting or broken and uneven, use a nail filer and correct the unevenness. Make sure there is no dirt under your fingernails by cleaning them with a nailbrush.

Others will want to be around you more when you keep yourself clean and fresh. These eleven simple points are all you need observe to maintain a healthy personal hygiene. With a healthy personal hygiene, you will feel more confident, self-assured, and successful.

Your dress and grooming - less critical than personal hygiene but a significant contributor to your self-image and thus your attitude, is your dress and grooming.

As the saying goes “if you dress like a bum, you will be treated like a bum.” If you are treated like a bum by most people you meet, you will believe you are a bum, and act accordingly. Your attitude will align with how you are perceived by others.

Hairstyle, nail care, the use of scents, and the actual clothes you select to wear, all say something about you.

What does yours say? Does it say what you would like to be seen as; does it represent the wonderful human being you are?

Fashion is difficult to advise on, as trends change so frequently. However, we all know when we are under dressed, or over dressed for a given situation. Whilst this type of mistake is embarrassing, it need not be a regular occurrence. You can avoid this by observing some simple rules for dressing and grooming:

1. Keep your clothes clean. Have them dry-cleaned or washed.
2. Remove wrinkles from your clothes by ironing them. When not in use avoid wrinkling and ironing by storing your clothes using clothes hangers to.
3. Keep your shoes polished and clean
4. Wear matching socks, stockings, tights etc.
5. Wear the right size clothes. Avoid sleeves that are too long or trouser legs that are too short.
6. Ladies, wear the correct bra size. It will save you a lot of pain and discomfort. Get measured professionally so that you can buy the size that supports you best.
7. Wear comfortable shoes. You will walk easier, and look more comfortable if you are not constantly worrying about the discomfort of your feet.
8. Wear a coat that suits your outfit. Avoid wearing leisure jackets over business suits and trench coats over casual leisurewear.
9. For men avoid silly ties in the corporate environment.
10. Red, Orange, and Yellow are warm colours whilst Green, Blue, and Violet are cool colours. In cold countries, use black or dark blue as your base

colours, and introduce warm colours, cool colours, or white in moderation. For help with occupational dress see *www.symsdress.com* for further information. You should also consult John T. Molloy's *New Dress for Success* and *New Women's Dress for Success*.

11. Avoid bright clashing colours. Each colour group works well with other colours in the same group. Whilst generally colours from different colour groups tend to clash and cause striking differences. Black and White tend to be neutral and generally work well with cool or warm colours.
12. Avoid caps or leisure head wear in the corporate environment.

    Keep your nails, hair, moustache, and beard well groomed. Consult a hairdresser or barber in this. This point has already been covered in the previous section, but it is repeated here as it pertains to your grooming.

Your environment - Victor Frankl, a Jewish concentration camp survivor observed, in his book *Mans Search For Meaning,* that although the concentration camp environment was designed to be soul destroying, there were some inmates, including himself, who kept a positive outlook, held on to their humanity, self esteem and positive attitude and survived.

This amazing man, and his incredible experience, is one example that you are not your environment, and no matter how bad your environment is, a positive mental attitude can help you maintain a positive self-image and self-esteem.

If you can change your environment by relocation, or some other means, then seek this solution first. However, if you cannot change your negative environment, then change your negative mental environment. It is said that, "if there are no enemies within then the enemies without can do you no harm". Therefore, first seek to cleanse your mind from all negative thoughts and beliefs. By doing this, you will realise that the negative environment has little, or no effect on your mind.

We have already discussed ways of cleansing your mind of negatives. Remember that in a dark room, it only requires the flick of a switch to end the darkness. Always keep that positive hope and faith whilst you search for that light switch in your times of darkness.

So to summarise, if your environment is bringing you down and eroding your positive attitude:

1. Determine what your choices are in minimising, eliminating, or moving away from the negative environment. If you can move away from the negative environment, take action immediately to end the positive attitude erosion (please note that suicide is not suggested here).
2. If you have limited choices in eliminating, or moving away from the negative environment, minimise the effect from associating with the environment by spending more of your time in a positive environment to compensate. You can create a positive environment within the negative environment where you can feel safer, securer, and happier.
3. If you have, no choices outside yourself at all as Frankl found in the concentration camp, then use your trump card. Make the choice to stay positive, optimistic, cheerful, and positive no matter what the external environment throws at you.

You do not have to apply only one of the three options given. You can apply all of them, or as many of them as is possible in your situation.

Material pleasure – plan and set goals to achieve your positive desires and dreams. Work towards things that will give you positive feelings and pleasure. Make sure the attainment of these things will not harm or rob others of their human rights. The areas to work on for material pleasure are as follows:

Achievements – your material achievements will bring you pleasure and improve your mental attitude

Dreams and goals – the journey towards a dream or goal is full of many vicissitudes, but the act of being on this journey alone will improve your mental attitude.

Reward – the rewards you give your self for the attainment of goals and tasks will also be a source of positive mental attitude. Make sure each goal you set, carries with it a reward for its achievement. These earned rewards bring more pleasure than rewards that are not earned.

Planning – the planning phase of any endeavour can be very pleasurable. Holiday planning, for instance, is exciting, and positively enjoyable. Make sure you are constantly working on a project, goal, or task. Plan these activities in detail, and execute your actions according to the plan.

Spiritual belief – believing in a higher power and knowing that this power is manifested in your daily life, can be a source of much joy, and can elevate your attitude sky high.

Discipline

Just as hard work is its own reward, discipline also rewards you through developing within you, a more focussed mind, and a stronger will. With increased focus of mind and stronger will power, you can maintain a positive mental attitude for longer periods, without distractions and backsliding.

To develop a stronger more focused mind and will, try:

- Meditation – meditation is the silencing of your conscious minds' chatter to allow contact to be made with a higher level of awareness or consciousness. Meditation can help you relax, sleep, or simply become more aware of yourself, and the Creator. Because meditation calms your minds' chatter, it allows you to better hear and identify the smaller, softer voices that speak to you. These voices have been made small from lack of being paid any attention. Profound truths can be learned, inner peace gained, and perfect solutions discovered, for your challenges when you calm your mind and listen internally. This inner peace promotes and supports a positive mental attitude.
- Abstaining -
  - Fasting – whether undertaken for religious reasons, or for health purposes, fasting benefits you by cleansing your body, strengthening your mind and will power. You can fast by abstaining from eating one day a week, one week a month, or one month a year. When you fast, make sure you drink a lot of water. There are many

types of fasts. You may choose to undertake a:

- Water fast – This is where you only drink water during the fasting period.
- Solids fast - This is where you only consume liquids during the fasting period.
- Fruit and vegetable fast – This is where you limit your consumption to only fruit and vegetables.
- Missed meal fast: This is where you miss a meal from your day (breakfast, lunch, or dinner).
- Dawn until dusk fast – This is where you abstain from all foods, except water from sunrise until sundown.

There are a few common sense medical issues to keep in mind:

- Consult your medical doctor before undertaking any fast.
- Avoid fasting if you are pregnant or ill in any way.
- Stop fasting if you start feeling dizzy or nauseous.

Fasting is a great way of staying in shape. When you fast, you allow your body to concentrate its resources on processing your previous meals, and cleansing itself from waste products, and detoxifying. Fasting also allows you to gain control and power over your body. This strengthens your will and focuses your mind.

- Delayed gratification – if you tend to buy whatever you want, whenever you want it even if you do not have the funds to afford it, you will not get as much pleasure from your purchases.

  If you bought luxury items after you had achieved a worthy goal and earned them, by working towards a goal, successfully achieving that goal on schedule and earning a reward for your efforts, you will feel great for the success, and you will feel like a winner when you are taking possession of your reward.

  Use delayed gratification with your non-essential but desired purchases. The waiting will be worthwhile as you will be achieving your goals, and working towards your dreams at the same time.

  When you do successfully earn the reward, the satisfaction will be sweeter, and the reward will have more meaning to you than if you had not delayed gratification.

  Delaying gratification also strengthens your will and helps focus your mind.
- Celibacy – abstaining from sex for a given period, or permanently, is challenging, and rewarding at the same time. Doing this builds mental toughness and strengthens your will power. Overcoming the control of these urges will make you a

happier more confident and self-assured person. Being happier and more confident will elevate your mental attitude.

- Silence – when you stop using a faculty, the remaining faculties will grow in strength. This is what happens when you decide to stop talking. Whether for a given period, or for the rest of your life, silence can be greatly rewarding in itself. Just as the other types of abstention we have discussed, silence offers inner peace, self-control, will power, and a sense of personal power.

If you can, get away to a quite place and be at one with yourself, God and the elements. Whether sailing, mountain climbing, rambling or simply meditating, short or long periods of silence are excellent for achieving inner peace and mastering your mind.

Chapter 4

- ***How to maintain and improve your positive attitude***

How To Maintain And Improve Your Positive Attitude

Children

Having children brings with it many challenges and many rewards. When you face these challenges with a positive attitude, you will increase the rewards of parenthood.

Your children are an extension of you and therefore, you treat them differently to how you would treat others.

When this treatment is positive, your children will grow up to be well adjusted. They will have respect for others and other people's property, love themselves, and strive to be better.

When this treatment is negative, your children will be maladjusted and exhibit, timidity, bullying, violence, verbal abuse, hatred, rebelliousness, and self abuse amongst other things.

It is therefore critical that you develop a positive attitude towards your children, and teach them to develop similar attitudes from an early stage of their lives. Help bring up a positive future by having a positive attitude, and help your family do the same.

There are many books on effective values based parenting; if you have not read any of them yet, then you can start with the following:

1. *Children Learn What They Live*
   By Dorothy Law Nolte

2. *How To Build Confidence In Your Child*
   By Dr James Dobson

Material Things

You may have some material possessions that affect a positive attitude within you. Whether a motorbike, car, clothing, or some other possession, if it inspires a positive attitude within you then, drive, ride, wear and make use of these possessions regularly.

When ever you are feeling a little down, or if you sense your attitude is flagging, go and use your favourite possession. Doing this will give your attitude an immediate boost

As you read earlier, all possessions are enjoyed more when shared, so try to incorporate sharing, whenever you use your favourite possessions. If you enjoy it by yourself, you will enjoy it even more when you share it with a friends, or family.

Have A Clearly Defined Vision, Dream, Objective, Or Task In Mind

Without vision, your life will have no purpose, without purpose you will have no reason to live. You can maintain a positive attitude, and regularly improve on it, by having a vision, a purpose, or a dream. You have a reason to live, which is why you are still alive. This means that you have a vision, a dream, or a purpose that is keeping you alive. Currently, this purpose may be vague and without definite objectives and measurable results.

If your dream or objective is not clearly defined, you will not know when to start or when to finish. You will exist in limbo living a life without a clear purpose, a life of mediocrity. You will be alive, but you will not be living. Without a life purpose, you will be like a ship without a rudder. You will be bounced between natural events, and the results of other people's actions. If this situation is prolonged, your attitude will decay into negativity.

This type of life is frustrating and disorientating. To gain control of your life, you must get a life vision, and clearly define your purpose, dreams, objectives, and tasks. A ship out of control is bounced from shore to shore. It is buffeted by the waves and sea currents. It has no clear destination or purpose. If lucky, it will wound up on a new shore, or worse, it will be shipwrecked on some desolate rocks.

Make sure your life does not run aground, or end up a wreck, on some rocky shores. Take control of the helm, and switch on the engines. Steer your life where you plan to end up. You can do this by asking yourself the following questions:

- What do I want my life to stand for?
- What do I want to achieve in my lifetime?
- Who do I want to be?
- What places do I want to visit?
- What people do I want to meet?
- What dreams do I want to achieve and live?
- What sort of person do I want t o become?
- Where do I want to live?
- How do I want to be viewed by others?
- How much do I want to earn or be worth?
- Whom do I want to help?
- Where do I want to be spiritually?
- How do I want my body, and health to be?
- What do I want to leave behind?
- Whom do I want to share my life with?
- What do I want to learn and know?

The questions above, and others like them, will help you to define the eight areas of your life. These are:

1. Spiritual
2. Family
3. Relationships
4. Health
5. Charity

6. Educational
7. Financial and career
8. Recreational and fun

Asking and answering questions that help define you, as you would like to be, will reveal to you what you want your life to define, and stand for. Knowing what your life stands for, will give you a life vision. From this life vision, you can develop your purpose, by defining tasks, objectives, and goals within each of the eight life areas, the achievement of which will create, and develop the sort of person that you want to be. By living the life you dream, your attitude will stay positive.

Making your dreams and objectives clearly defined

Before you move on to look at the planning stage, which is covered next, let us see how you can clearly define your dreams, objectives and tasks. To define your dreams, objectives, and tasks, is to determine the essential quality of them. The attributes that best define your dreams, objectives, and tasks must all be clearly listed.

As an example, if your dream is to be wealthy. You would clearly define this dream by specifying the exact amount that having, would represent being wealthy to you. Being wealthy also implies an associated lifestyle. So clearly define this lifestyle.

Do you want to own land, corporations, investments, or a mixture of all of these? Do you want to be popular, or to retain your privacy, and be relatively unknown? What luxury items do you want to own? What charities do you want to fund? What cars, boats, yachts, private jets, helicopters, racehorses, sports teams, real estate, clothing, holidays, and recreational toys etc do you want to have at your disposal?

Your dream of being wealthy is now more definite. You will definitely know when you have achieved it, and you can break its achievement down into smaller components. These could be as follows:

- Building the businesses to generate the funds to acquire the lifestyle.
- Saving and investing to generate the funds to acquire the lifestyle.
- Reaching the financial figure at which you would achieve your dream of being wealthy.
- Acquiring the trimmings (cars, boats, jets etc…)

Each one of these points can be divided into smaller subgroups. For example, if having a net worth of £10,000,000 and cash in the bank value of £1,000,000 would, mean you are wealthy, then this objective can be subdivided as follows:

1. Increase net worth to £50,000, with £5,000 cash, in the bank.
2. Increase net worth to £100,000, with £10,000 cash, in the bank.
3. Increase net worth to £250,000, with £25,000 cash, in the bank.
4. Increase net worth to £500,000, with £50,000 cash, in the bank.
5. Increase net worth to £750,000 with £75,000 cash, in the bank.
6. Increase net worth to £1,000,000 with £100,000 cash, in the bank.
7. Increase net worth to £2,500,000 with £250,000 cash, in the bank.
8. Increase net worth to £5,000,000 with £500,000 cash, in the bank.
9. Increase net worth to £7,500,000 with £750,000 cash, in the bank.

10. Increase net worth to £10,000,000 with £1,000,000 cash, in the bank.

From the main objective of having a net worth of £10,000,000, and cash in the bank, valued at £1,000,000, you now have ten incremental objectives. This gives your plans a stepping-stone to build this wealth on. As the saying goes, divide and conquer. This is particularly true for goal setting.

Repeat this objective division process for all your dreams and your large long-term objectives. This process is not suitable for tasks and short-term objectives as they may already be small enough not to require it. An example of this is the task to mow your lawn. This single task is simple, and small enough not to require further division into smaller tasks. Doing this would be a waste of your time.

Meticulously plan the achievement of your goal

Now you know what you would like to achieve within the eight areas of your life, you can begin to plan how to make the transition from you, as you are now, to you, as you will become when you are living your definition.

The process for translating dreams and objectives into reality is called goal setting, and goal achievement. We shall now look at the goal setting process in detail. Goal achievement will be covered later. Suffice to say, without goal setting, you will not be able to execute goal achievement.

Setting goals

Once you have a clearly defined dream or objective, you can proceed to the planning stage. This stage is where you categorise your objectives into long, medium, short term and tasks. This process works best if you start from long term, and work towards tasks, rather than the other way around.

The purpose of this exercise is to:

1. Help you gain balance in your life, by having an even spread of goals in the eight areas of your life, over the different periods (long, medium and short term).
2. Identify similar objectives, so that you can later, maximise your resource usage.
3. Break down large complex objectives into task sized components.
4. Generate a goal for each objective. Remember, a goal is an objective with an assigned deadline date, and an appropriate reward for its successful achievement.
5. Provide a visual representation of the progress of your objectives, as they relate to each other.

Let us take a closer look at these four period categories.

Long term

The long-term category is for all objectives that will require two or more years to achieve. You can place all your high abstraction visions, purposes, dreams, and objectives here. Examples of things to include are, to climb Everest, to be a millionaire, to own a McLaren F1, or to become a pop star. You should have already, subdivided these types of dreams and objectives during the process of making them clearly defined.

Lifetime objectives and dreams should all be included here. The subdivided objectives for each of your lifetime objectives and dreams can be moved to the medium or short-term categories, as and when required and necessary.

Medium term

The medium-term category is for all objectives that will require six months to two years to achieve. You should move all appropriate subdivided objectives for each of your lifetime objectives and dreams here.

Short term

The short-term category is for all objectives that require less than six months to achieve. You should move all appropriate subdivided objectives for each of your lifetime objectives and dreams here. Subdivided medium term objectives should also be placed here.

Tasks

This is where you should place the smallest non-divisible objectives. These tasks should be expedited within a week.

Although a task is small and simple, it may be time sensitive and thus require you to wait until the appropriate time before you execute it.

An example is, waiting to set your video to record your team play in the finals. You will have to wait until you know your team has made it through the quarter and semi finals before you set the video.

Therefore, although setting the video is a relatively simple task, you will have to wait for weeks, before you know if you can execute the task or not.

A linked process

Each category in this process helps define and affects the others. Any changes in the definition of your objectives at this stage will filter through all the categories, and affect all the other dependent objectives. This is the reason why, you clearly defined your objectives earlier.

Dating

To have a successful rendezvous, you will need to have these key details:

1. The meeting place.
2. The time and date.

Similarly, you already have your version of the place. This is your objectives. You now need to set the time. Just as the place had to be clearly defined, the time too has to be clearly defined. For most goals, a day of the month, month, and year will suffice. In rare cases or for most tasks, the second, minute and hour will also be required.

There are two ways to determine what time and date you should select for your deadline. These are:

1. By external restriction. For example, if your train leaves at five o'clock, and it will take you ten minutes to get to the station, your objective will have an externally restricted deadline of 4:45. It is suggested that you give yourself an extra five minutes to catch the train in case you are delayed.
2. By internal restriction. This is a self-imposed restriction. You decide when you feel you can comfortably achieve the objective, and set that as your goal deadline.

External restrictions are normally inflexible. If you miss them, you will fail in achieving your goal. Internal restrictions are only as inflexible as you decide to make them. It is suggested that you make them as inflexible as the external restriction option, until you fail in achieving the goal. Only then should you reset the deadline date.

There is a reason for this. This reason is that if your deadline is fluid, you will constantly move it, and delay the goals achievement, whilst if the deadline date is rigid, you will have to change something else, mainly your efforts.

Every dream, objective, and task should have a deadline date and/or time associated with it. Unless your objectives have deadlines, they are not goals.

We will now look at the final part of creating a goal, the reward.

Reward success

When you have something to gain from a task, you are more committed, dedicated, and enthusiastic. Failure ceases to be an option, the more you desire the reward for achieving a goal. It is therefore important to assign a desired reward to every goal.

In some cases, the achievement of the goal itself is the desired reward. An example of this is, if you set a goal to travel to Venice from 1st May 2007 to 7th May 2007. Achieving this goal will mean, you get to go to Venice in the first week of May 2007. That trip is the reward and the goal all rolled into one.

In most cases however, the reward needs to be independent of the goal. This is especially true when, what you have to do to achieve the goal is unpleasant, difficult, or undesirable.

When deciding on rewards, there are a few rules to bear in mind. These are as follows:

1. Always assign a reward to each goal.
2. Make sure you assign a highly desired reward.

3. Create rewards by using delayed gratification and abstinence.
4. Never make the reward larger than the goal. For example, if your goal is to earn £10,000, do not assign a reward costing £12,000. This defeats the purpose of the goal. Your reward should never exceed ten percent (10%) of the value of the goal.
5. Court the reward. Have pictures of the reward around your home. If the reward is externally based, go and visit it, smell it, touch it, spend time with it, to increase your desire for it.

Let us expand points 3 and 5 further.

Abstain

If you are finding it a challenge to assign rewards to your goals, use things you currently are attached to, and abstain from them until you have achieved your goal. As an example, if you love riding your motorbike in the weekends, then abstain from riding your motorbike until you have successfully achieved your goal.

Delayed gratification

If you normally gratify your wishes as and when you have them, choose to delay gratification for some wishes until you have achieved your goal. An example, if you decide to pay off your mortgage within five years (as you can learn to achieve from my book, *How to destroy your debt*), and you want to have a fitted kitchen installed, you could delay having this kitchen fitted until you have cleared the mortgage on the house. The fitted kitchen would be your reward for achieving the goal of paying off your mortgage on time.

Delayed gratification is ideal for those of you who love shopping (retail therapy). You can delay shopping, or delay purchasing a desired item, until you have successfully achieved your goal.

When your enthusiasm wanes, simply visit the item you want to own, and familiarise yourself with why you are working to achieve the goal.

This type of courting (a.k.a. dream building), is highly advised when working with rewards. Go and see the reward. Familiarise yourself with it. Imagine how it will feel to own and use it. Actively build your desire for the reward, and you will increase your chances of successfully achieving your goal.

This technique is used everyday for the sole purpose of minimising discomfort during childbirth. Mothers do not focus on the inconveniences associated with childbirth, instead they think of their child, what it will be called, how it will feel to hold, feed, play with, and all the other joyful things that babies bring.

Use this technique with all your goals, and you will greatly increase your chances of successfully achieving every goal you set.

Acquire The Resources For Your Plan

To achieve every goal, certain resources are required. Whether this resource is you, a notepad and a pencil, or a consultant, tax advisor or a priest, you cannot avoid having to work with resources for the achievement of your goals. If you have to work with resources, it is a great idea to maximise your efficiency and productivity in doing so.

Not all resources are the same. Some are expensive, free, temperamental, agreeable, unreliable, dependable, dangerous, safe and everything in-between. In some cases, managing different resources requires experience, tact, common sense, and specialised knowledge.

To know the skills you will need to handle different types of resources, let us first examine the different types of resources:

1. Low cost material items (pen, notepad, rubber, neck tie etc)
2. High cost material items (computer system, electro mechanical devices, real estate etc)
3. Low cost human aid (friend helping for free or for a fee, family helping for free or for a fee etc)
4. High cost human aid (doctor, consultant, technician, guide, psychologist, etc)
5. Difficult non human aid (awkward animals, plants, ice, perishable food etc)
6. Dangerous items (dangerous animals, firearms, explosive chemicals, flammable chemicals, acids, unstable structures etc)

General advice for all resources

- Whenever possible, acquire your resource at rock bottom price.
- If feasible, buy in bulk and resell the surplus for a profit.
- If you are inexperienced in acquiring, managing, storing, and handling a resource, seek professional help.
- Pay for professional handlers and trainers/keepers whenever working with dangerous animals.
- Utilise all resources to their full potential. Waste not and you will want not.

Advise for handling human aid

When dealing with human resources, your ability to relate, communicate, and command respect, will stand you in good stead. To this end, you must learn and use interpersonal skills (a.k.a. skills with people or people skills).

What Is A People Skill?

People skills are a set of tools and rules for handling human-to-human relationships effectively. By learning and applying these skills, you will be effective, productive, and successful at dealing with other people.

The basis of all people skills is love and respect. When you treat others with love and respect, you will receive the best response from them. You must always remember that the most important person in anyone's life is himself or herself.

People skill works with this knowledge, and teaches you to treat all others with respect. People are individuals, and therefore they are as important as you are. Treating others courteously, listening to them when they speak without interrupting, and using their name and second person pronouns in conversation with them, will get you far.

Why You Need People Skills

Other people can help you achieve your goals through giving you some of the following:

1. Physical help.
2. Financial help.
3. Moral support and encouragement.
4. Ideas.
5. Contacts.
6. A break.

Let us look at each of these points in more detail.

Giving you physical help

Often your goal requires manual labour to make it a success. This is true if you are redecorating your home, landscaping your garden, clearing out an attic, mending your car etc. Often the help of a family member, friend, or associate will mean success or failure in completing a project. If you do not know how to approach, and ask for this help in the most effective way, you will not get this help, and your project will fail.

Giving you financial help

Often the success of a business or the purchase of a home, amongst other goals, requires the generosity of a financial backer. Whether it is for a mortgage, a loan, or a donation, people skills could mean the failure or success in obtaining this financial help.

Giving you moral support and encouragement

You will have periods when your enthusiasm and spirit wanes. This is especially true after a major setback. It is during these times that you need moral support from your family, friends, or others. If you do not use people skills, and therefore, you upset and drive all your potential supporters from you, you will be alone and have to cope by yourself, through these difficult times. You may not be able to cope and give up due to lack of hope or through a broken spirit.

Spiritual nourishment will do more for you than almost any other type of nourishment. Do not underestimate the support that others can give you. Make sure this support is available to you when you need it, by always using positive people skills when dealing with others.

Giving you ideas

If you have ever reached a dead end whilst working on achieving a goal, you will know the importance that other people, with helpful ideas, play in the attainment of any success. You do not have to do it all alone; working with others will accelerate your success and save you valuable time and money. Again, people skills play a key role in attaining this help. People like to help and/or work with those they like. Using positive people skills, you can become amiable and effective when dealing with others.

Giving you contacts

Often someone will point you to a resource that has the answer you are looking for. This answer could be the key element required to achieve success in a particular goal. These contacts will save you time, money or simply help you increase your vision, and thus the size of your results.

Here is an example of such help. Initially, the plan was to write only one book. However, a friend pointed out a resource that allowed for quicker publishing, and at a fraction of the price of a conventional publisher. With this new resource, this book and over twenty more were penned in less than twenty-four months.

That is the power of contacts. They can save you time, money and refuel your enthusiasm.

Giving you a break

Often when you are working on a project, you will need to deal with some less than helpful individual in a position of power. Successfully working with this person will determine your projects success or failure. An example of this could be, working with the local planning officer when you are applying for planning permission for an extension to your property, or a self-build property plot.

These are the times when you need a break. Getting this break will require skills with people and patience. Without both of these, you are doomed to failure in getting the willing help of most people.

Obstacles To Effective People Skills

You now know why you need people skills, but what stops you from having it now? The following are why most people have not developed effective people skills:

1. They are ignorant of the need for developing people skills.
2. They do not know how, or where to learn these skills.
3. They do not believe these skills work, and thus they are not prepared to invest time learning them. This is normally due to laziness, as these people often have never learned and applied these skills, and thus are assuming, rather than making an intelligent judgement
4. Having learned people skills for their work, some people confine its usage solely to their job. These people have not made the connection between people skills and every aspect of their life.
5. Some people have learned people skills but they use it to manipulate others. Using people skills like this will make you look like an insincere fake. This will eventually make people distrust you, and anything you have to offer.

Positive people skills work, and are the most effective way of dealing with others. Positive people skills will get you through the door when your status, power, and credentials fail. Therefore, learn and use positive people skills in every aspect of your life.

How To Improve Your People Skills

You will now look at how you can develop, and employ people skills in your life.

Positive people skills can be used everyday and everywhere, to make your days, and others lives, more pleasant. When used this way, it will pave your way for success with people when you really need them. This is a worthy investment, as it benefits everyone.

The following are ways of using people skills in every day situations with people you deal with:

1. Setting peoples moods.
2. Talking with people.
3. Listening to people.
4. Agreeing with people.
5. Making people feel important.
6. Thanking people.
7. Praising people.

Let us take a closer look at these seven points.

Setting peoples moods

Before you speak to someone, before you shake his or her hand and exchange greetings, use your greatest tool of disarmament, your sincere smile. This tool will melt most people's hearts, and make them more receptive to you. The following is how to utilise your smile effectively:

1. Smile sincerely whenever you make eye contact with people.
2. Smile sincerely and maintain eye contact until they reciprocate the smile or they break eye contact.
3. Think nice thoughts about the person at whom you are smiling. This makes it easier to smile sincerely.
4. During your time, or conversation with them, be quick to smile. Smile often, and always sincerely.

Work on this one skill, sincere smiling. It will open many doors and defrost many welcomes for you.

Talking with people

When talking to people, keep them at the centre of the conversation. Use the second person pronoun "you", "your", "yourself" and "yours", more than you use the first person pronoun "I", "me", "my", "myself" and "mine".

Whenever possible use names. Ask people their preferred name, and only use this. Learn people's names by using it frequently in conversation. People like the sound of their own name. Hearing their name used makes people warm to the speaker.

Get others to talk about them by asking them an open-ended question[2] about themselves. When they are talking about themselves, listen with interest, and do not interrupt. During the conversation, ask questions that show you are listening. This will get others to carry on talking about themselves. You will look more at listening in the next section.

In every conversation, aim to have others talk more than you. You already know all about yourself. Therefore, talking about yourself will not teach you anything new. Listening to others talk about themselves however, will reveal a lot to you, and teach you much about them.

Listening to people

There are a few points to observe when listening to others. To become a great listener, you should pay close attention to these points. These points are as follows:

1. Look at the speaker.

---

[2] An open-ended question is one that cannot be answered with a one or two word answer. These questions normally include the request for another's opinion. For example, "How do you feel about this company?"

2. Physically lean towards the speaker. If possible make sure your whole body, especially your feet are pointing towards the speaker.
3. As previously mentioned, ask questions to show you are listening, and are still interested.
4. Do not interrupt the speaker. Allow them to dictate the topic they want to discus.
5. Use you, your, yours and yourself, as well as the speakers preferred name when conversing with them.
6. Do not fidget, scratch, cough, or otherwise distract and irritate the speaker.

Agreeing with people

Everyone likes to think he/she is right most of the time. They therefore like to be agreed with. If you are a person who agrees and are agreeable with people, they will tend to like you, and tend to like being around you. Conversely, if you are a disagreeable person, and tend to disagree with people often, you will find yourself alone most of the time. People will tend not to like you, or to like being around you.

To become more agreeable and to agree more with people, observe the following:

1. When you agree with someone, verbalise it. Tell them you agree with them. In conversation, use the word(s) "yes", "you are right", and "true".
2. Be the first to admit when you are wrong.
3. Do not verbalise to people that you disagree with them, unless doing so will save a human life. Do not disagree if you cannot agree. Refuse to argue or fight. It takes two or more parties to sustain a conflict. Do not be one of the parties.
4. Learn to be agreeable. This will make you more approachable. People will feel safe around you, and will entrust you with their personal confidences.

Making people feel important

The best way to get the most out of people is to treat them with respect; to make them feel important. To do this you will need to observe the following points:

1. Use their preferred name, and when possible, use picture(s) or their creations, such as their art, music, corporations etc, when addressing them.
2. Use the second person pronoun "you", "your", "yours", and "yourself", when talking to people. Use these words more than "I", "me", "mine", "my", and "myself".
3. Listen attentively when people speak. See the listening to people section on page 67 for more details.
4. When asked a question, pause first before answering, so that you are seen to be listening, and to have thought about their question first.
5. When people earn or deserve it, applaud and compliment them. Do this whether they are present or not. Hearing that you were complimenting them behind their backs will really get people to like you.
6. Show those waiting for you, or waiting to see you, that you are aware they are waiting. Apologise for making them wait, and give them a timeframe in which you will be free to see them.
7. In a group, pay attention to everyone within the group. Smile, and make eye contact regularly with each of the group members.

Thanking people

You like to be thanked, and so too does everyone. Thank people when they help you, or when they help others. Thank people when they do anything courageous, good, noble etc. Thank people for listening, for sharing, for caring, for coming, for understanding, for supporting, for remembering etc.

If you think about it, you will realise there is almost an endless list of things you could thank people for. Seek these things and thank people for them. Here are a few points on effective thanking:

1. Say it sincerely.
2. Say it clearly, so all present can hear.
3. Use their preferred name when thanking people.
4. Look at those you thank. Make eye contact when you say "thank you".

Praising people

There are many people in the world doing a fine job as parents, or in their job, but are not being praised enough for it. Be a praise giver. Seek out people in situations worthy of praise, and give them their praise.

There are seven main rules for praising people. These are as follows:

1. Give them eye contact.
2. Be sincere.
3. Use their preferred name.
4. Use second person pronouns such as, "you", "your", "yours" and "yourself".
5. When praising them alone, praise the person.
6. When praising them in front of others, praise the act, and not the person (this is to avoid embarrassment, or others thinking you are showing favouritism).
7. Be quick to give praise. Actively look for opportunities to give out praise.

Using people skills to disarm aggression

There are several scenarios where you can use positive people skills to disarm. These are:

1. When making introductions. To make a good first impresssion, simply give eye contact and smile sincerely.
2. When making a complaint, compliment first, make the complaint next then compliment again. For example, "Tom, thank you for working so hard this last year. I would like to ask you to come to work on time from now on. You have done great things for this company. Let us not tarnish such a great record with poor attendance, Tom".
3. When you are receiving a complaint, do not interrupt, listen intently, maintain eye contact, apologise sincerely for the complaint, admitting to your fault, where necessary.
4. When in a debate, confrontation, or argument, refuse to fight or argue. If you are unable to agree, do not disagree.
5. In situations where you want to influence others:

    - Listen carefully to what they want.
    - Rephrase what you want, according to what they want, showing them how they can get what they want by giving you what you want.

    When selling an idea or goods, always use third person pronouns. This is because:

    - They sound more sincere and believable than the first person pronouns do.
    - People like to buy through referrals and personal recommendations.

    Selling to them via third person utilises this knowledge. As an example, if you were selling your car and the prospective buyer asks if it is economical to maintain, recall a true statement, like how your mechanic complains about the money he is loosing out on because your car never breaks down.

To influence and convince others:

- Ask yes questions whilst subtly nodding your head.
- Give people a choice between several yeses,
- Expect them to say yes.

6. When criticising:

   - Select a private location where no one can overhear.
   - First, sincerely compliment the person on something.
   - Follow this with the criticism of their action.
   - Ask for their corporation in this matter in the future.
   - End with another compliment or kind word.
   - Only discuss one incident per criticism.

   When you are being criticised:

   - Do not interrupt,
   - Listen intently,
   - Maintain eye contact,
   - Admit to your fault and apologise sincerely for the criticism when necessary.
   - Do not argue or fight.

Execute your plan immediately

As you can see, acting on your plans comes immediately after planning and goal setting. The wording of the previous sentence was deliberate. "acting on your plans comes immediately after…" The immediacy of execution, will add momentum and value to the achievement of your goals. This is called goal achievement.

Without goals, your actions will not be focused, coordinated and effective. It is in the execution of a precise plan, to achieve a definite goal, that action should always be directed. Therefore, if your plans are not precise, and your goals are not definite, it is suggested you return to the planning and goal-setting sections, reread them, and apply them properly.

Do it now

Once you know what to do and how to do it, you should do it immediately. As the Nike slogan says, "Just do it". Procrastination will rob you of momentum, enthusiasm, confidence, and impact. By acting immediately, you strike whilst the iron is hot.

Your goals will require immediate action in order to maximise your chances of successfully achieving them. From applying for a coveted job, to catching the last train of the day, immediacy of action plays a critical role in successfully achieving your goals. By delaying, procrastinating, or vacillating on taking action, you are choosing to delay the achievement of your goals. Choose to succeed, by taking action NOW.

Journal your success

Keep copies of your plans and goal setting. It is good, from time to time, to review your successes, doing this will add to your positive attitude. Keep a journal or a diary. Diaries are a source for self-analysis, and a key resource for documenting your life.

Often you cannot see the progress you are making in the improvement of your positive attitude. By keeping a journal or a diary, you can have visual evidence of this progress. Rereading your diary will shed light on where you have improved, and on where you need to concentrate on for future improvements.

Spiritual Belief

Praying allows you to make a connection, through your faith, with the Creator. Sometimes in the game of life, it can seem like you have been dealt a bad hand. It is during these times that you should pray, and renew your relationship with the Creator. Visiting your place of worship, praying, and studying with fellow believers, is advised for renewing and rebuilding your faith.

With strong spiritual faith, you will worry less, and pass all issues that are out of your control to the Creator. What little you are left with, will be manageable by you. Living like this alleviates a lot of worrying, and stresses, allowing you to more easily, maintain your positive attitude.

Visualisation

How do you see yourself? Can you picture yourself acting and living with integrity? Use mental pictures to strengthen your self-image. Visualisation is the process by which astronauts, high achievers, athletes, and sportsmen use to see themselves winning before it actually happens. You can adopt this technique for strengthening your integrity and gaining success in the clean out of your bad habits.

Sit or lie somewhere quite and peaceful. Clear your mind of chatter, and picture yourself, as you want to be. Imagine yourself in situations where you want to have more integrity. In the mental pictures, see yourself acting with total integrity. Feel how it will feel like. Do this at least once when you awake, and again when you retire to bed. Very soon, you will be living the mental pictures that you visualised.

Reframing

Neurologists have made phenomenal breakthroughs in understanding how the mind creates and maintains reality. It is now widely accepted that each one of us has, created in our minds, a reality that is unique only to us, and is based on our interpretations of our life experiences.

Two people can experience the same event, but see and feel differently about the event in their minds. This will be based, not on the experience alone, but on the experience as seen, felt and understood from their frame of mind.

This concept of a frame of mind has being expanded on by neuro-linguists over the last half a century into a field of study called Neuro-Linguistic Programming (NLP). This field is constantly growing, and our understanding of the changes we can achieve from reframing our thoughts, memories and language is constantly growing with NLP.

In this section, you will learn a simple technique for reframing your thoughts in order to change your attitude.

To get started, find a quite peaceful moment in your busy day, in a quite peaceful place. This could be in bed, in the bath or even whilst travelling on the metro to work. Close your eyes and picture yourself, as you would like to be i.e. happy, fulfilled, attractive etc.

How is the picture framed? Is it:

- In a frame or is it frameless?
- Filling the whole image or is it only taking up a portion of your vision?
- To one side of your vision or the top or bottom of your vision?
- Still or a moving image?

- Coloured (are the colours vivid or dull); black and white or faded like those old pictures from the early 19th century?
- A sunny happy background or a dull grey dark and moody background?
- Heavy or light?

If you could:

- Taste the picture, what would it taste like? Sweet, Sour, or another flavour?
- Smell the image, what would it smell like?
- Feel the picture, what texture would it be, hard, soft, smooth, rough, or a mixture?

What is your frame of reference? Are you:

- Viewing the picture from outside? Is it at a distance or close up (are you viewing it straight on, from above from below, from the left or the right side?)
- In the picture? Is it panoramic or totally surrounding and engulfing you?

Now you will take your positive picture and reframe it. To do this, simply change the various attributes we have already touched on. Here is a summary of these attributes:

1. Boundary
2. Size
3. Reference point
4. Motion
5. Colour
6. Background
7. Weight
8. Taste
9. Smell
10. Feel

These ten attributes are controllable, and you can use your mind and imagination to manipulate them to create a new image of yourself.

Now you have your current self-image in mind, begin to change the various attributes as follows:

1. ***Boundary***; remove boundaries from your picture. You should remove all frames and enclosures from your image of yourself.
2. ***Size***; increase the size of your picture so that it fills your whole vision no matter where you turn. It should completely surround and engulf you.
3. ***Reference point***; move your reference point from viewing the picture to actually being the person in the picture.
4. ***Motion***; make your picture be active and moving like a movie. If there are trees, sea, breeze, or any movement in the background, experience it in the picture. See the trees swaying, birds flying, and feel the breeze and smell the flowers etc. If you are interacting with others in the picture, see yourself confidently doing so, and see them responding in the way you want, i.e. with interest, admiration, enthusiasm, adoration, love, respect etc.
5. ***Colour***; make all colours vivid and vibrant in your picture. Use bright colours that make you fell good and happy.
6. ***Background***; set the picture against a background that brings you the most joy and happiness. Examples of these could be at a paradise island beach, or a barbeque with your family or friends. The setting of your best memory is best to use for this.
7. ***Weight***; experiment with lightness and heaviness to determine which weight, when associated with the picture, makes you feel best. Once you have determined which, make the picture feel that way (light or heavy).

8. ***Taste***; if you could taste the picture, what taste would you feel most happy with your image having? Apply this taste to your image.
9. ***Smell***; if you could smell the picture, what smell would you feel most happy with your image having? Apply this smell to your image.
10. ***Feel***; if you could feel the picture, what texture would you feel most happy with your image having? Would it be silky smooth like velvet or more like glass, rough like the skin of an orange or more like steel? Experiment with different textures (soft, hard, rough or smooth, cold or hot, and everything in between) until you have one, or a combination, that makes you happiest with the image. Apply this texture to your image.

When you have completed this picture, step into it and let it engulf you so that it is you and you are it. Now whenever you think of yourself see this image of yourself and feel the new you.

This exercise is great because once you have created the image, you can always return to it instantly just by thinking of yourself. You do not need to go through this process of creating the image, every time, after the initial reframing exercise.

Your Self-Talk

The words you use to describe yourself are very powerful, and they reinforce your attitude negatively or positively. If you find yourself constantly deriding and badmouthing yourself for being clumsy, stupid, dumb, ugly, lazy etc, you will affect your attitude negatively.

So how can you change this situation?

You can use positive self-talk techniques to program your mind subconsciously whilst you drive, iron, or even sleep. To do this you will need a tape recorder, MP3 recorder, or any music and voice recording device.

Making your own self talk program

The steps to creating your own self-talk program are follows:

1. Select some positive, instrumental easy listening, or instrumental soft classical, music. It is vital that the music is soft, instrumental (contains no human voices), and the music makes you feel good.
2. Draft a list of positive statements about yourself. These statements should be:
    - stated in the first person ("I am")
    - stated in the present tense ("I weigh 190 Pounds")
    - positive ("I breath clean air and my lungs are clean and healthy")
3. Record your statements over the instrumental music. Whilst the instrumental music is playing in the background, state your positive statements, clearly and in a relaxed tone.
4. Make copies of the resultant recording and play this recording in your car or whilst you sleep.

It does not matter if you do not consciously listen to the recording. As long as you can hear the recording in the background, your subconscious mind will hear, and take its instructions from the recording subconsciously.

How does this work? This works because you have a part of your mind that monitors all inputs to your brain at all times. You are only aware of what you hear, see, feel, and taste because of your minds ability to filter out the vast majority of inputs from your conscious mind.

You can put this to the test by looking out for red cars the next time you are driving. You will notice that you spot an alarmingly increased amount of red cars. Why is that? It is not because the numbers of red cars have increased after you decided to look out for them; rather it is because you instructed your mind to filter out all other colours except red.

Your subconscious mind does the same for all your senses. Only bringing to your conscious attention items and events you may be interested in, or have specifically requested to be informed about. This is the reason that new mothers can hear the tiniest sound that may warn them of dangers to their newly born babies.

The filtered information is not discarded by the subconscious mind; it is simply not made immediately available to the conscious mind. Therefore, your self-talk will be processed by the subconscious mind, and the statements will be digested, and acted upon even though you may not consciously be aware of this going on.

So if you play a recording of positive self-affirming statements. You will start consciously seeing and feeling the results of this recording in the way you see yourself and the way you are perceived by others.

Showers

Taking a cold shower is a great way to raise your attitude. It is almost impossible to take a cold shower without acting like a little child. Because of the coldness of the water, your skin will receive a shock sensation from the cold. You will immediately speed up your movements, as you want to complete the event as quickly as possible. When it is over, you will feel absolutely refreshed, invigorated, and alert.

This tool is best used when your attitude is being negatively affected by torpor. In such states of inertia, a sensual shock works best to shake you out of the inactivity.

Please do not use this technique if you are ill or suffer from any medical condition that a cold shower will aggravate, or worsen.

Warm Baths

Taking a slow relaxing warm bath (with or without the ambience of candles and scented incense), will relieve stress and anxiety. You can use your favourite bath salts, bath oils, or bubble bath soaps to heighten the enjoyment of the warm bath.

Soaking in a warm bath relaxes your muscles and eases tension and stress, as well as slowing the pace of your thoughts, allowing you to, temporarily, forget your worries.

Vacation

Occasionally you will need to get away from your busy life, to recuperate your mind and body. Taking a vacation is one of the best solutions for achieving this. Vacations allow you to remove yourself from your normal environment or routine, and to do something different for a while.

Whether you are climbing a mountain, napping on a beach in paradise or helping feed refugees in a war torn country, a break will be required in your life from time to time. A good vacation will positively refuel your attitude, and give you plenty of good feelings and memories to replay during less favourable times. Try to take a short break every quarter (3 months). This could be a weekend break, or a week or more away from your normal routine and environment.

When on vacation do not allow negativity to creep into your mind, or the vacation scenario. Be upbeat, and look for ways to enjoy your vacation more. If something negative does occur, deal with it quickly, and resume the enjoyment of your vacation. Do not allow anything to ruin your vacation by causing you to have a negative attitude.

Massage

To help relieve stress or just to feel pampered, go for a massage, or get someone you know to give you a relaxing, stress relieving massage. A good massage will relieve stress from your muscles, and get lymph (cell waste), moving through your body.

You will feel good on the outside, and benefit from the lymph drainage from the inside. You will leave with a more positive attitude after a good massage.

There are many types of massages, keep trying them all until you find the one that you like the most. The following is a list of massage types:

- Acupressure
- Craniosacral Therapy
- Deep Tissue Massage
- Lomi Lomi
- Lymphatic Drainage
- Myofascial Release
- Neuromuscular Therapy
- Orthopaedic Massage
- Petrissage
- Pregnancy Massage
- Raindrop Therapy Reflexology
- Reiki
- Rolfing
- Seated Massage
- Shiatsu
- Sports Massage

- Stone Massage
- Structural Integration
- Swedish massage
- Tapotement
- Thai Massage
- Trager
- Trigger Point

Love Making

Few things will change your mental attitude quicker than sexual pleasure. Sex can be a great tool for changing your mental attitude, if you have a willing partner, and you take the appropriate precautions for safe sex. Good sex will relieve stress, diffuse aggression, and negative feeling, whilst creating a closer bond between you and your partner.

There is a great difference between sex and lovemaking. Sex focuses on the physical act whilst, lovemaking encompasses sex but goes further to introduce a spiritual element, love. After making love, a couple will feel closer together, and more in love with each other, whilst after sex, a couple will simply be sexually satisfied.

Aim to make love with your partner rather than simply having sex. Your love life will be more fulfilling, and you will attain a level of closeness that will last, and add to your positive mental attitude.

Conclusion

You can have a negative or positive mental attitude. Your mental attitude plays a vital role in your success and happiness in life. If you have a negative mental attitude, failure, and misery will be your lot in life. You will have few true friends and experience alienation, from others. No one likes to be around someone with a negative mental attitude. If you have a positive mental attitude, you will draw people to you and turn your failures into successes. People like to be around someone with a positive mental attitude.

You have learned how to identify negative mental attitudes, and their root causes, as well as positive mental attitudes and their root causes. You have learned how to develop and maintain your positive mental attitude.

To help you develop and maintain a positive mental attitude, you have been given techniques for the following:

- dealing successfully with people,
- planning,
- goal setting,
- creating your own self talk recordings, and
- changing your thoughts and feelings through reframing,

Choosing to develop your positive mental attitude, and working to further improve, and maintain it, will change the results you experience from your decisions, conversations, how you feel about yourself, and your dealings with others.

I pray that you choose to use the advice and lessons in this book to shape, and change your mental attitude so that you can better your life, and the lives of all who associate with you.

Notes

Other Works By Samuel Blankson

How to Destroy Your Debts

Printed: 165 pages, 6.0 x 9.0 in, Perfect-bound
Download: PDF (1739 kb)
ISBN: 1-4116-2374-6
Copyright Year: © 2005 by Samuel Blankson
Language: English
Publisher: Lulu.com

If you are like me, you hate being in debt! Every month you watch, your money run out before the end of the month. You scrape around for fuel and grocery money, and then finally you hit the credit cards, hoping they hold sufficient funds.

If you want to get out of this cycle of worry over debt, this book may be your answer. I say, “May,” because although this book will definitely give you techniques for controlling, managing, and even getting out of debt altogether, it will not do the work for you. That will be up to you.

This book will reveal how to destroy your debts, including your mortgage. It will also make clear to you how you can increase your income, and have confidence in your financial future. Your journey to financial freedom begins here.

The Practical Guide to Total Financial Freedom: Volume 1

Printed: 124 pages, 8.5 x 11.0 in, Perfect-bound
Download: PDF (7761 kb)
ISBN: 1-4116-2058-5
Copyright Year: © 2005 by Samuel Blankson
Language: English
Publisher: Lulu.com

The first part of a five volume series on creating Total Financial Freedom. In this volume, you will learn the foundations of wealth building, and how to secure your family and your wealth against disasters and losses.

This series offers practical, effective, and easy to follow advice for securely and quickly building wealth. If you are thinking of buying this book, you probably want to be free. Free from the rat race, free from the boss, free from the wage trap, and free from the mediocrity and hopelessness of poverty and lack of options. Until now, you may have had no other way of achieving this within the next half a decade.

This book will change all that forever. This book, unlike many self-help books out there, will actually tell you what to do in order to achieve Total Financial Freedom. You will find out exactly how I went about achieving Total Financial Freedom. If you read, learn, and apply the lessons in this book, you too will achieve Total Financial Freedom.

The Practical Guide to Total Financial Freedom: Volume 2

Printed: 173 pages, 8.5 x 11.0 in, Perfect-bound
Download: PDF (31040 kb)
ISBN: 1-4116-2057-7
Copyright Year: © 2005 by Samuel Blankson
Language: English
Publisher: Lulu.com

The second part of a five volume series on creating Total Financial Freedom. In this volume, you will learn how to invest in Bonds, Stocks and Shares, and Funds.

This series offers practical, effective, and easy to follow advice for securely and quickly building wealth. If you are thinking of buying this book, you probably want to be free. Free from the rat race, free from the boss, free from the wage trap, and free from the mediocrity and hopelessness of poverty and lack of options. Until now, you may have had no other way of achieving this within the next half a decade.

This book will change all that forever. This book, unlike many self-help books out there, will actually tell you what to do in order to achieve Total Financial Freedom. You will find out exactly how I went about achieving Total Financial Freedom. If you read, learn, and apply the lessons in this book, you too will achieve Total Financial Freedom.

The Practical Guide to Total Financial Freedom: Volume 3

Printed: 143 pages, 8.5 x 11.0 in, Perfect-bound
Download: PDF (1716 kb)
ISBN: 1-4116-2056-9
Copyright Year: © 2005 by Samuel Blankson
Language: English
Publisher: Lulu.com

The third part of a five volume series on creating Total Financial Freedom. In this volume, you will learn how to invest in En Primeur Wine, Real Estate, Businesses, Life Insurances, Art, and Offshore investment opportunities.

This series offers practical, effective, and easy to follow advice for securely and quickly building wealth. If you are thinking of buying this book, you probably want to be free. Free from the rat race, free from the boss, free from the wage trap, and free from the mediocrity and hopelessness of poverty and lack of options. Until now, you may have had no other way of achieving this within the next half a decade.

This book will change all that forever. This book, unlike many self-help books out there, will actually tell you what to do in order to achieve Total Financial Freedom. You will find out exactly how I went about achieving Total Financial Freedom. If you read, learn, and apply the lessons in this book, you too will achieve Total Financial Freedom.

The Practical Guide to Total Financial Freedom: Volume 4

Printed: 134 pages, 8.5 x 11.0 in, Perfect-bound
Download: PDF (3961 kb)
ISBN: 1-4116-2055-0
Copyright Year: © 2005 by Samuel Blankson
Language: English
Publisher: Lulu.com

The fourth part of a five volume series on creating Total Financial Freedom. In this volume, you will learn how to trade and invest in Momentum products. These instruments are high-risk products that offer high returns, but also the possibilities of high losses.

You will learn how to limit those losses by reducing the risk using effective and practical methods. Options, Futures, High Yield Investment Programs, and Gambling are some of the exciting topics covered in detail. This series offers practical, effective, and easy to follow advice for securely and quickly building wealth.

This book, unlike many self-help books out there, will actually tell you what to do in order to achieve Total Financial Freedom. You will find out exactly how I went about achieving Total Financial Freedom. If you read, learn, and apply the lessons in this book, you too will achieve Total Financial Freedom.

The Practical Guide to Total Financial Freedom: Volume 5

Printed: 322 pages, 8.5 x 11.0 in, Perfect-bound
Download: PDF (7143 kb)
ISBN: 1-4116-2054-2
Copyright Year: © 2005 by Samuel Blankson
Language: English
Publisher: Lulu.com

The last part of a five volume series on creating Total Financial Freedom. In this volume, you will learn how to lower your taxes, avoid paying unfair and unnecessary taxes, and how to move offshore and pay no taxes at all.

This series offers practical, effective, and easy to follow advice for securely and quickly building wealth. If you are thinking of buying this book, you probably want to be free. Free from the rat race, free from the boss, free from the wage trap, and free from the mediocrity and hopelessness of poverty and lack of options. Until now, you may have had no other way of achieving this within the next half a decade.

This book will change all that forever. This book, unlike many self-help books out there, will actually tell you what to do in order to achieve Total Financial Freedom. You will find out exactly how I went about achieving Total Financial Freedom. If you read, learn, and apply the lessons in this book, you too will achieve Total Financial Freedom.

Living the Ultimate Truth, 2nd Edition

Printed: 166 pages, 6.0 x 9.0 in, Perfect-bound
Download: PDF (855 kb)
ISBN: 1-4116-2375-4

Language: English
Publisher: Lulu.com

Today most people live a poor example of a balanced life. The centuries of wisdom passed down from the great leaders of our past seem lost amid lives centred on minutia and selfishness.

Today we care more about what we wear and where we are seen, than we do about discovering and Living the Ultimate Truth. Throughout the world, there is an imbalance in people's spirituality, consciousness, and inner harmony. This has taken a great toll on our environment, our health, and our happiness. Many are wondering around like lost sheep, seeking a shepherd in all the wrong places.

Many false prophets have promised quick fixes to these problems, but if these solutions are not firmly rooted in The Creator, love, integrity and inner harmony, they are doomed to fail.

This book is a reminder of all those virtues and universal principles that we need, to return to a balanced, harmonious, and happy life. You will learn to love yourself, love others, and finally find that inner peace you seek through spiritual growth.

Developing Personal Integrity, 2nd Edition

Printed: 118 pages, 6.0 x 9.0 in, Perfect-bound
Download: PDF (627 kb)
ISBN: 1-4116-2376-2
Copyright Year: © 2005 by Samuel Blankson
Language: English
Publisher: Lulu.com

In the field of human character development, integrity is the last frontier. Many people use the word, but few really know what real integrity is.

This book breaks down the fundamental components of personal integrity and offers a path to attaining it. Like success or happiness, integrity is a journey not a destination.

We can only measure how far on the path we are through the observation of our inner voice, the voice of our conscience, and through deep contemplation and reflection.

This journey of personal excellence is not an easy one, and as a friend once said, “When peeling this onion, sometimes you cry.” Nevertheless, in all great endeavours, the harder the struggle, the greater the victory will be.

The Guide to Real Estate Investing

Printed: 117 pages, 6.0 x 9.0 in, Perfect-bound
Download: PDF (723 kb)
ISBN: 1-4116-2383-5
Copyright Year: © 2005 by Samuel Blankson
Language: English
Publisher: Lulu.com

If you have ever wanted to know how to make money from real estate, but could never find one source that listed and explained all the different options available to you, then your search is over.

This book covers over 20 different ways of investing in real estate. You will find the author's style easy to understand and very practical. The section on self-build is so in-depth, that after reading it you will actually know how to build a house, and the section on REITs, Indexes, and REIT Options will leave your mind boggling at the potential profits available to you.

This book also covers the conversional and popular methods of real estate investing as well. Therefore, whether you want to learn to develop real estate projects, build your own home, or simply rent a room in your house, this book will help you maximise your success and avoid the pitfalls.

Tax Avoidance A practical guide for UK Residents

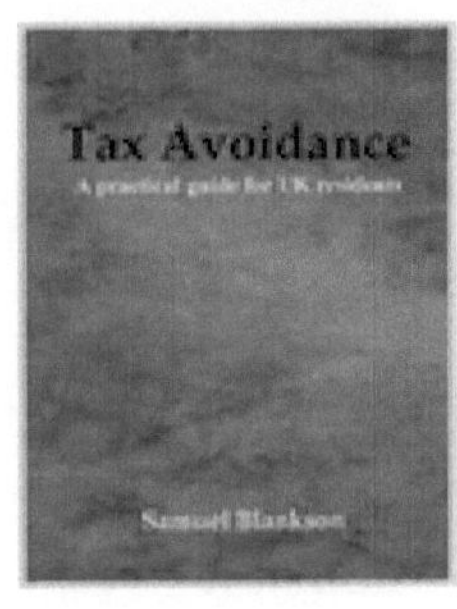

Printed: 104 pages, 6.0 x 9.0 in, Perfect-bound
Download: PDF (355 kb)
ISBN: 1-4116-2380-0
Copyright Year: © 2005 by Samuel Blankson
Language: English
Publisher: Lulu.com

UK residents pay some of the highest taxes in the world. Most of these taxes are hidden through VAT and service charges. This guide clearly explains what taxes you are paying, and which ones you can and should avoid paying through claiming your allowed deductions and allowances. Prudent tax efficient estate planning is explained in detail, and hundreds of tax saving ideas are shared within these pages. Whether you are a qualified accountant or a non-professional, you will find this little guide an invaluable source of tax saving ideas and strategies.

Making Money with Funds

Printed: 79 pages, 6.0 x 9.0 in., Perfect-bound
Download: PDF (8769 kb)
ISBN: 1-4116-2671-0
Copyright Year: © 2005 by Samuel Blankson
Language: English
Publisher: Lulu.com

Today the world fund market is a multi trillion-dollar industry. There are many types of funds and as many reasons for choosing them. In this book, you will learn how Funds work, and how you, can make money with them.

How to make a fortune with Options trading

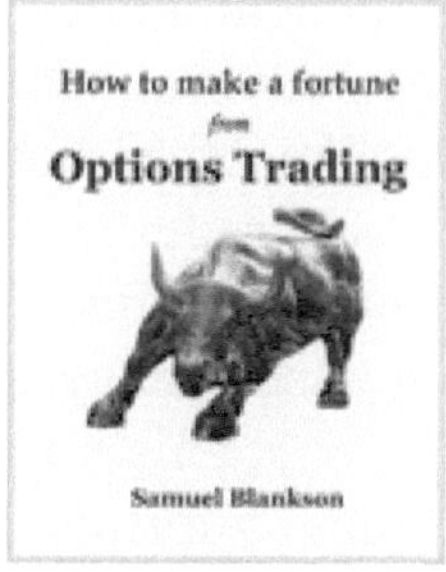

Printed: 59 pages, 8.5 x 11.0 in, Perfect-bound
Download: PDF (1808 kb)
ISBN: 1-4116-2378-9
Copyright Year: © 2005 by Samuel Blankson
Language: English
Publisher: Lulu.com

This is a practical book on winning in the Options trading market. Whether you are a sophisticated investor or a complete novice, this book is for you. The author takes complex ideas, and explains them in a way that is both practical and easily understood by anyone. Having used these techniques to achieve financial freedom, Mr Blankson now shares with you how he did it. There is no waffling here, just plain speaking and powerful techniques that anyone can apply.

How to make a fortune on the Stock Markets

Printed: 190 pages, 8.5 x 11.0 in, Perfect-bound
Download: PDF (8769 kb)
ISBN: 1-4116-2379-7
Copyright Year: © 2005 by Samuel Blankson
Language: English
Publisher: Lulu.com

This book contains simple but effective techniques for achieving regular and consistent profits from stock trading. Unlike other books on the topic, it is not full of theory and projections, but practical advice learned the hard way, by trading personal hard-earned cash daily in the world's stock exchanges. Moreover, unlike other books on the subject, it is not about how to be a stock trader and trade other people's money, but on how to grow your own funds to a level where you will never have to work for anyone else again.

This book contains real techniques used by the author to amass a fortune significant enough to have made him Financially Free. Now you too can use these simple but highly effective techniques to achieve the same results. Therefore, whether you are a professional trader or a total beginner, this book will show you how to achieve Financial Freedom through trading Stocks and Shares.

Attitude

Printed: 418 pages, 6.0 x 9.0 in, Perfect-bound
Download: PDF (13700 kb)
ISBN: 1-4116-2382-7
Copyright Year: © 2005 by Samuel Blankson
Language: English
Publisher: Lulu.com

Attitude, so often misunderstood, yet so vital for success in every aspect of our lives. A positive attitude will guarantee happiness in your life, promotion, and growth in your career or job, peace and joy in your family life, and in addition, a positive attitude has been scientifically proven to help extend your life expectancy. In this book, this essential success attribute is explained in detail. You will learn how to safeguard against positive attitude erosion, and learn how to build a positive mental attitude to help you achieve measurable success in every aspect of your life.

How to Win at Online Roulette

Printed: 81 pages, 6.0 x 9.0 in, Perfect-bound
ISBN: 1-4116-2570-6
Copyright Year: © 2005 by Samuel Blankson
Language: English
Publisher: Lulu.com

This is a guide to consistently winning at online Roulette. It is a simple and to the point writing about an amazing system for gaining an advantage at online Casinos. This book will show you how to make £1000 per day or more from online Roulette.

The Ultimate Guide to Offshore Tax Havens

Printed: 418 pages, 8.5 x 11.0 in, Perfect-bound
Download: PDF (12602 kb)
ISBN: 1-4116-2384-3
Copyright Year: © 2005 by Samuel Blankson
Language: English
Publisher: Lulu.com

This book is a detailed listing of all the known and not so commonly known Tax Havens, their benefits, and their suitability for relocation by the low tax seeker. If you are looking for ways to cut your taxes, there is no better way than to relocate to a low or no tax haven. The South East Asian Tsunamis and earthquakes have shown us that it is prudent to select the haven you will reside in carefully. Low taxes cannot be your only gauge for this task. This book will help you make that decision.

A must read for all who aspire to changing their lifestyles by relocating offshore. The havens are listed in geographical order, starting with the USA and ending with the South Pacific Islands.

How to win at Greyhound betting

Printed: 68 pages, 8.5 x 11.0 in, Perfect-bound
Download: PDF (639 kb)
ISBN: 1-4116-2377-0
Copyright Year: © 2005 by Samuel Blankson
Language: English
Publisher: Lulu.com

Today, sports betting is a big industry for the bookmakers and organisers. Of all the people who benefit from sports racing, the "punters" (or in this case, you), are the last on the list of people who consistently gain. In fact, the greyhounds probably gain more from these races than most punters. Why is that? Well, there are many reasons, but most of them centre on these two things: lack of a proven system, and greed. This book closely examines these two points, and offers techniques and systems for achieving consistent wins in greyhound betting.

Images of Kilimanjaro

Printed: 53 pages, 8.5 x 11.0 in, Perfect-bound
Download: PDF (2573 kb)
ISBN: 1-4116-2016-X
Copyright Year: © 2004
Language: English
Publisher: Lulu.com

This is a book of pictures taken from Kilimanjaro. This is an accompanying book to the Calendar of the same name.

The Ultimate Greyhound Betting System

Download: MS Excel (233 kb)
Copyright Year: © 2005 by Samuel Blankson
Language: English
Publisher: Lulu.com

If you think there is no trustworthy betting system out there, then prepare to be proven wrong. This is the betting system described in the series *The Practical Guide to Total Financial Freedom,* and the book *How to win at Greyhound betting.* This semi-automatic system allows its user to achieve a minimum of 30% profits per week by following a proven statistical and rule based system betting on UK Greyhound races. The system only requires you to supply the race results and place the bets with your bookmaker. Armed with this incredible system, you will be able to beat the odds, and win one over the bookmakers.

Sixty Original Song Lyrics

Printed: 200 pages, 6.0 x 9.0 in, Perfect-bound
Download: PDF (1072 kb)
ISBN: 1-4116-2059-3
Copyright Year: © 2004 by Samuel Blankson
Language: English
Publisher: Lulu.com

This is a compilation of original song lyrics by Samuel Blankson. This book contains 60 of the songs he wrote in between 2000 – 2002. Having had some of these lyrics made into songs for an album (see *www.practicalbooks.org*), and several of them now on compilations, Samuel now shares these 60 song lyrics with you.

Images of Kilimanjaro

Printed: 26 pages, 11 x 8.5 in, Coil-bound
Start Date: January 1st, 2006
Duration: 12 months
Copyright Year: © 2004 by Samuel Blankson
Language: English
Publisher: Lulu.com

Kilimanjaro, the tallest freestanding mountain in the world, is captured here for you to feast your eyes on each month through 2006. Kilimanjaro is a source of life for Tanzania and Kenya locals, who live on its life giving rains and water. I had the honour of climbing this majestic mountain, and captured the essence of its allure and mystery through these pictures.

Uju

Download: MPG (6523 kb)
UPC: 4-3157-3526-2
Copyright Year: © 2004 by Samuel and Uju Blankson
Language: English
Publisher: Lulu.com

A six track EP with soulful R&B tracks with a pop flavour. This EP is bound to have you humming along addictively. For more info about the artist Uju, visit *www.uju-music.com* and look out for her forthcoming album.

The Bass by Samuel Blankson

Download: MPG (4811 kb)
Copyright Year: © 2004 by Samuel and Uju Blankson
Language: English
Publisher: Lulu.com

A sexy, R&B track with wicked beats and a deep baseline. With a melody and chorus that will stay with you for a long time, this addictive and catchy tune deserves your download (see *www.practicalbooks.org*).

Investing in En Primeur Wine

Printed: 88 pages, 6.0 x 9.0 in, Perfect-bound
Download: PDF (1,095 kb)
ISBN: 1-4116-2867-5
Copyright Year: © 2005
Language: English
Publisher: Lulu.com

Wine investing is not new, it has been going on for centuries. In more recent years (the last two centuries), government tax laws on alcoholic drinks have made buying wine a little more prohibitive to the investor who wants to keep them at home in his/her private cellar. Nevertheless, as usual, the market has found a way around this problem.

You can avoid taxes and V.A.T. (Value Added Tax) by buying fine wine on Bond (also called wine Futures or En Primeur). This book covers a simple and effective way in which anybody coming into the fine wine investing market place can safely securely and successfully select, and invest in En Primeur Wine.

Eight Steps to Success

Printed: 105 pages, 6.0 x 9.0 in, Perfect-bound
Download: PDF (1,095 kb)
ISBN: 1-4116-2738-5
Copyright Year: © 2005
Language: English
Publisher: Lulu.com

We would all like to live a successful life, a life where our relationships and finances are a source of happiness and joy. This life is attainable by following timeless success principles. These principles have been forgotten by our fast food, fast-paced, reality TV society.

This book defines, explains, and shows you how to apply these principles and skills in your life to attain happiness, contentment, peace, joy, and prosperity. The eight fundamental virtues and skills required to succeed long-term in any endeavour, are explained in detail and in a style that everyone can understand and immediately apply.

The Eight Steps to Success is an inspirational book that will help you understand, acquire, hone, and apply the principles of success.

Taking Action

Printed: 105 pages, 6.0 x 9.0 in, Perfect-bound
Download: PDF (1,095 kb)
ISBN: 1-4116-2735-0
Copyright Year: © 2005
Language: English
Publisher: Lulu.com

This is a book about taking action. For some, taking action means something you will do, might do, should do, have done, or never will do. This book will show you how to change your understanding of taking action to mean something you are doing NOW! When you change this focus in your life, you will release great powers. This book will show you how to tap into this phenomenal power and change your life.

Paris 2006

Printed: 73 pages, 8.5 x 11.0 in., Coil-bound
Download: PDF (12103 kb)
ISBN: 1-4116-3691-0
Copyright Year: © 2005
Language: English
Publisher: Lulu.com

Romance, love, chic, fine dining, all these can be found in abundance in Paris, the city of lights. Through the pictures in this enchanting book, you will always be reminded of the charm and beauty of Paris.

Images of Kilimanjaro In Colour

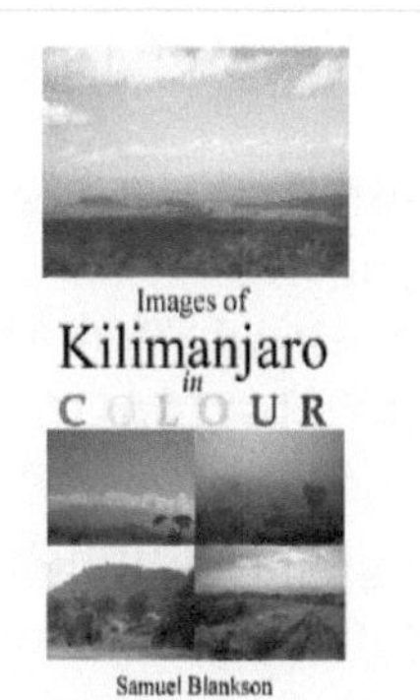

Printed: 73 pages, 8.5 x 11.0 in., Coil-bound
Download: PDF (4093 kb)
ISBN: 1-4116-3680-5
Copyright Year: © 2005
Language: English
Publisher: Lulu.com

When you are climbing Kilimanjaro, you will get very familiar with "Pole Pole". The Phrase uttered by your guide means "slowly slowly" in Ki-Swahili. As you look at these beautiful pictures of Africa's tallest mountain, that phrase comes to mind. You just cannot help but take it slowly for the rest of the day. This mountain has that sort of effect on you, and these pictures have captured this tranquil majestic beauty for you to savour all through the year.

The Heart of Moscow (Calendar)

Printed: 26 pages, 11 x 8.5 in., Coil-bound
Copyright Year: © 2005
Language: English
Publisher: Lulu.com

The heart of Moscow is captured here in these glorious pictures. Each picture shows a different side of this mysterious and historically rich city. Now you can enjoy the heart of Moscow with each passing month through 2006.

The Heart of Moscow

Printed: 73 pages, 8.5 x 11.0 in., Coil-bound
Download: PDF (8417 kb)
ISBN: 1-4116-3684-8
Copyright Year: © 2005
Language: English
Publisher: Lulu.com

The heart of Moscow is captured here in these glorious pictures. Each picture shows a different side of this mysterious and historically rich city. However, far from showing you the sites of Moscow, these pictures have captured the mysterious essence that is Moscow today.

Paris 2006 Calendar

Printed: 26 pages, 11 x 8.5 in., Coil-bound
Copyright Year: © 2005
Language: English
Publisher: Lulu.com

Romance, love, chic, fine dining, all these can be found in abundance in Paris, the city of lights. Through the enchanting pictures in this calendar, you will be reminded of the charm and beauty of Paris all through 2006.

Planning and Goal Setting For Personal Success

Printed: 200 pages, 6.0 x 9.0 in., Perfect-bound
Download: PDF (12103 kb)
ISBN: 1-4116-3774-7
Copyright Year: © 2005
Language: English
Publisher: Lulu.com

This book is about planning and goal setting to achieve success in the eight areas of your life. These areas are as follows:

1. Spiritual
2. Family
3. Relationships
4. Community
5. Charity
6. Educational
7. Financial and career
8. Recreational and fun

By learning to develop your dreams into achievable objectives with a time limit and associated reward for its achievement, you will create goals. Acting on your goals will bring success into your life. Working in all eight areas of your personal life will give you balance, harmony, and happiness. If you have not read this fantastic book, your life is loosing out on successes you deserve.

About The Author

An entrepreneur at heart, Samuel Blankson blends art, creativity, passion, business acumen, and financial expertise with careful planning and execution in the achievement of measurable results. He is an avid reader, writer, researcher, and securities trader.

He is an advocate of self-empowerment and an individual's ability to control their destiny through the achievement of personal freedom from economic, financial, spiritual, social, mental, and interrelationship restrictions. Samuel is constantly working to push the boundaries of personal achievements to their limits, recognising that these limits are only self-imposed.

Samuel has authored over twenty books (*How to Destroy Your Debts*, *Living the Ultimate Truth*, *Developing Personal Integrity*, *The Practical Guide to Total Financial Freedom* volumes 1, 2, 3, 4 and 5, and *Attitude* are some of these works). He has written over 100 songs, sixty of which are featured in *Sixty Original Song Lyrics*. He writes poetry, creates artwork, and works daily to express his creativity in many ways.

Having successfully run several businesses, Samuel diversified into securities trading over a decade ago, with great success. After learning from the masters of the time, Samuel progressed to develop his own methods and systems for successful trading. Today, he trades many financial instruments and has developed ways of successfully generating profits from his many investments.

A firm believer in knowledge sharing, Samuel travels the globe, teaching and sharing his personal knowledge with groups of friends, associates, and anyone who seeks to improve their life. This is the spirit of Samuel Blankson, a God centred philanthropist, overcomer, and high achiever.

www.ingramcontent.com/pod-product-compliance
Ingram Content Group UK Ltd.
Pitfield, Milton Keynes, MK11 3LW, UK
UKHW041937190726
13854UKWH00004B/1639